ALTO SAXOPHONE FINGERING CHARTS

Kimber Books

ISBN: 978-1-969068-03-4
© 2025 The Martin Freres Company, Merimax, LLC
All Rights Reserved

Thank you!

Thank you for choosing Alto Saxophone Fingering Charts, Scales & Songs. This book is designed for the E♭ Alto Saxophone and serves as a reference guide for beginners and developing players.

Inside, you'll find fingering charts, scales, and familiar songs arranged to make learning both visual and musical. You can start anywhere, and there is no set order to follow.

Some scales and songs are easier, while others reach higher into the saxophone's range and may take more time to master. This book is meant to stay with you as you grow, serving as both an introduction and a lasting reference as your skills expand.

Each song includes a QR code that links directly to its audio recording. Listening before you play helps you hear how the notes fit together and develop your sense of tone and timing.

We hope this book becomes a steady companion on your musical journey, one you can return to often whether you're playing your first notes or exploring new challenges.

Happy playing!

Martin Freres

the
MARTIN FRERES COMPANY
MartinFreres.net

Let's Begin

Learning to play the E♭ alto saxophone can feel tricky at first, especially when trying to figure out which fingers to use for the notes on the page. That's why this book has fingering charts right below each note. These charts make it much easier to focus on playing instead of guessing. Here's how to use them.

Understand the Fingering Chart
Each note comes with a fingering diagram that shows you exactly which keys to press.

- **Black keys** mean you should press those keys.
- **White keys** mean those keys stay untouched.

The fingering chart shown here is used for all the scales and songs in this book. On the music staff, the names of the notes are written above the staff to help you know what to play. Under each note, you'll see a fingering diagram that shows you where to put your fingers on the saxophone. This makes it easier to match the notes to the proper finger positions.

Notes to Play:
Letter above - Note below

E♭ Alto Saxophone Fingering

For each note, press only the keys that are solid black.

By using the E♭ alto saxophone fingering charts, you'll learn faster and have more fun playing, now!

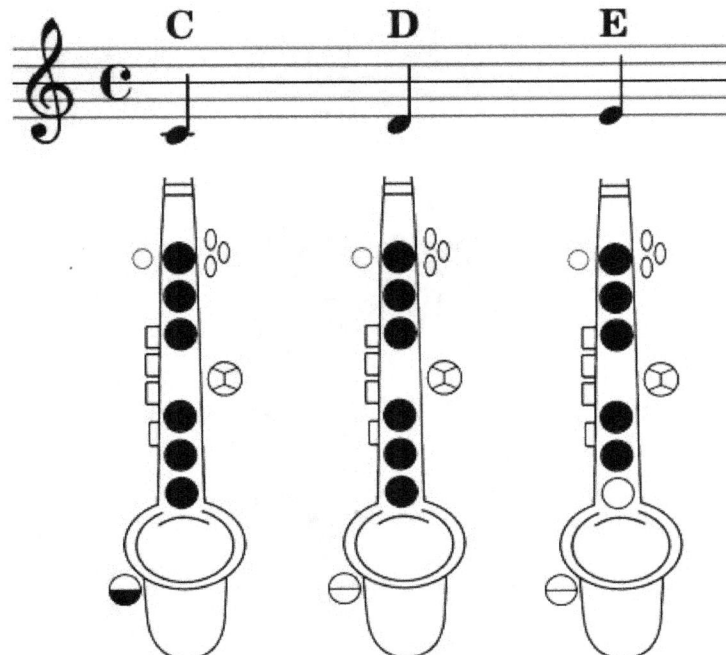

E♭ Alto Saxophone Fingering

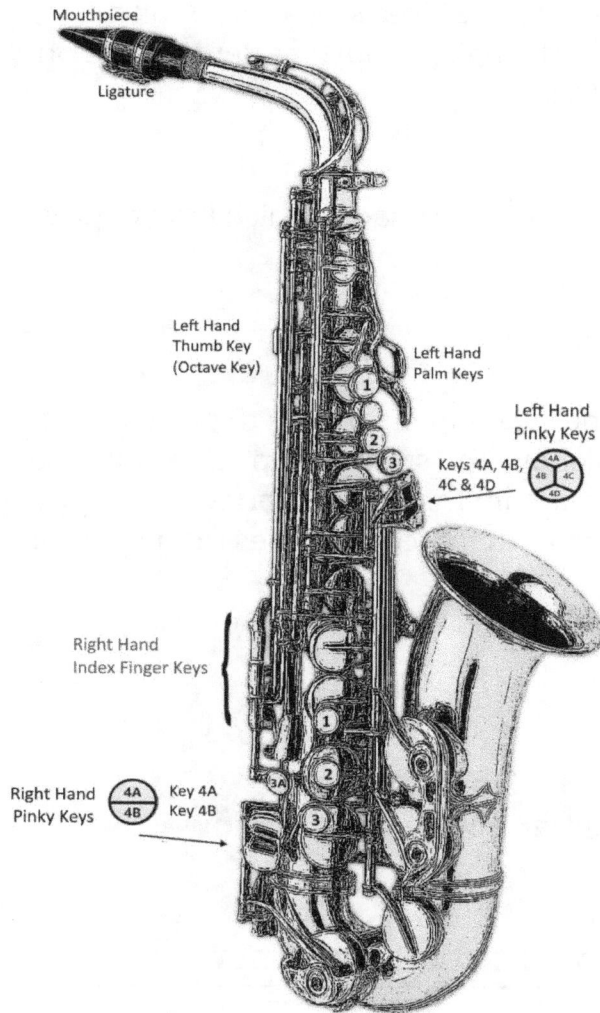

Which Finger Goes Where?

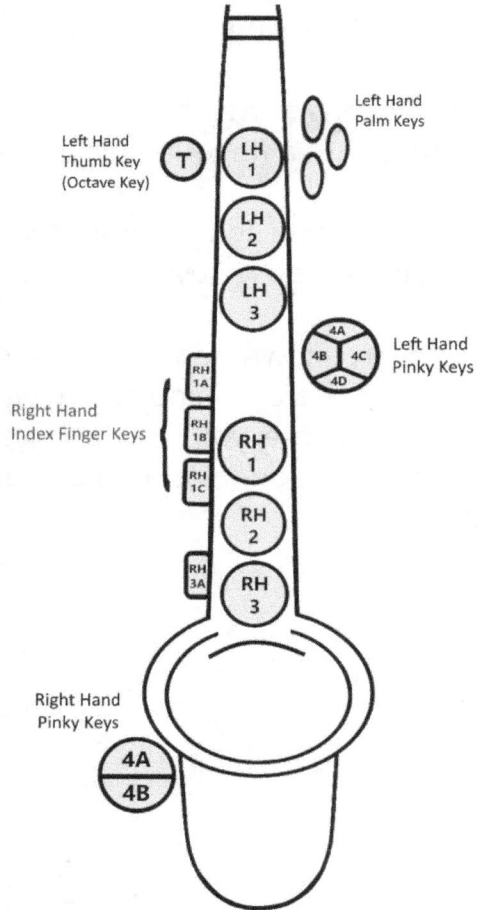

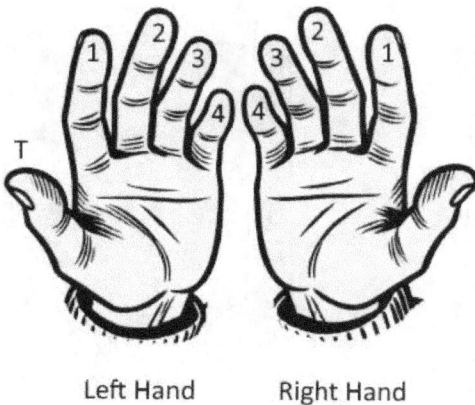

Mouthpiece

Ligature

Left Hand Thumb Key (Octave Key)

Left Hand Palm Keys

Left Hand Pinky Keys

Keys 4A, 4B, 4C & 4D

Right Hand Index Finger Keys

Right Hand Pinky Keys

Key 4A
Key 4B

Left Hand Thumb Key (Octave Key)

T

LH 1

LH 2

LH 3

Left Hand Palm Keys

4A
4B 4C
4D

Left Hand Pinky Keys

Right Hand Index Finger Keys

RH 1A

RH 1B

RH 1C

RH 3A

RH 1

RH 2

RH 3

Right Hand Pinky Keys

4A
4B

Left Hand

Right Hand

LH = Left Hand
RH = Right Hand

T = Thumb
1 = Index Finger
2 = Middle FInger
3 = Ring Finger
4 = Pinky Finger

TIP: Start with your left hand on top and your right hand on bottom. The thumb rests on the back thumb rest to press the octave key.

Learning to Play Alto Saxophone

Practice Scales First
The scales provided in this book are a great way to get used to the notes and their fingerings. Play through each scale slowly, making sure you match the note on the page with the correct fingering on your saxophone. Practice them until you can play smoothly without needing to check the fingering every time.

Use the Charts While Learning Songs
When you start playing songs, keep using the fingering charts as a guide. Play one note at a time and check your fingers if you need to. After a while, your fingers will begin to remember where to go, and you can follow the music sheet instead of the fingering charts.

Listen for Accuracy
Even if your fingers are in the right spots, your sound might still not be quite right if your breath control or mouth positioning (embouchure) isn't right. Use the charts to make sure your fingers are correct, but also focus on creating a clear, steady sound for each note.

Move Away from the Charts
As you get better, challenge yourself to play scales and songs by looking only at the notes on the staff. Let your fingers do the work from memory. The more you practice this way, the more confident and independent you'll become.

Use the Charts When You Need Help
If you're struggling with a note or forgetting a fingering, don't worry, just look at the fingering charts. They're there to help you when you need a quick reminder.

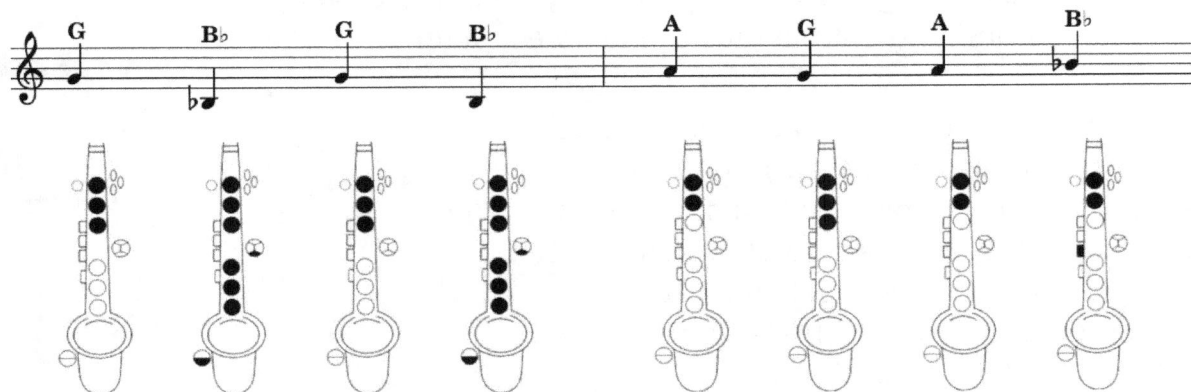

By practicing with these charts and gradually using them less, you'll build strong skills faster and with less frustration. Always remember, the goal is not just to play notes, it's to make music. With time and effort, you'll be playing with confidence and having fun.

Scales for Alto Saxophone

Major scales are like the building blocks of music. They're the foundation for nearly every song you hear, whether it's a pop tune, a movie soundtrack, or classical symphony. For E♭ alto saxophone players, mastering major scales helps you build strong fingers, improve your tone, and play with confidence. Since the alto saxophone is an E♭ instrument, the notes you read and play sound different from the ones on a piano. For example, when you play a C on the sax, it actually sounds like an E♭ on the piano. Pretty cool, right?

Why do we learn scales? Well, scales teach your fingers to move smoothly between notes, which is important for playing fast or tricky parts in songs. Scales also train your ears to recognize the sound of each key, making it easier to play melodies and harmonies in tune. Think of it like learning the alphabet before writing stories. It's hard to create music if you don't know the *language* of scales!

Here's a bit of history:
Scales have been around for centuries and were first written down by musicians in ancient Greece. The major scale we use today became popular in the 1600s and 1700s when composers like Bach and Mozart used it to write their music. When you practice your scales, you're following in the footsteps of musicians from hundreds of years ago. Plus, the better you know your scales, the more prepared you'll be to play solos, join bands, or even compose your own music.

Climb Higher!
Musical scales are like the steps of a ladder, helping you climb higher in your musical skills. Each rung shows how practicing scales builds your ability to play songs and understand music, one note at a time.

We begin with the C Major Scale. The C major scale is often the first scale musicians learn because it's the simplest, it has no sharps or flats, just natural ♮ notes (C, D, E, F, G, A, B, and back to C). On the saxophone, this scale helps you get comfortable with finger patterns and smooth transitions between notes. It's like the starting line for your musical journey, giving you a solid foundation to build on. The C major scale is a great way to dive into playing real songs.

So, grab your sax and let's start PLAYING NOW!

C Major Scale (Low)

Practicing the C major scale trains your ear to recognize the sound of a major key, which is important for playing songs and understanding how music works. The C major scale includes the notes C, D, E, F, G, A, and B. These notes are used to play many of the songs in this book.

Each note comes with a fingering diagram showing you which keys to press.

- Black keys mean you should press those keys.
- White keys mean those keys stay untouched.

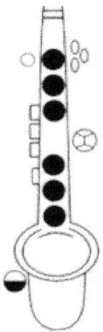

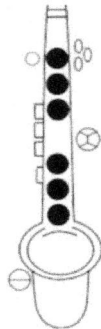

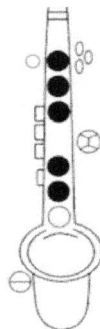

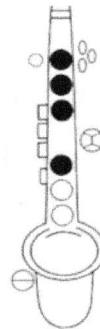

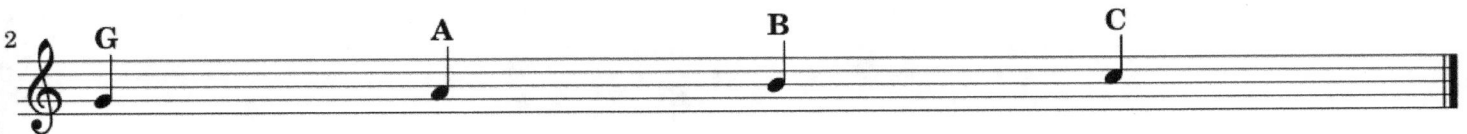

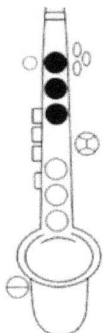

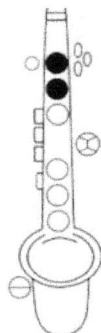

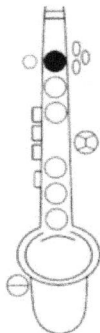

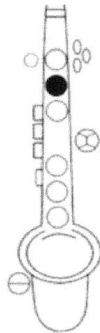

C Major Scale (High)

Here is the C major scale (high). You play the same notes as before (C, D, E, F, G, A, B) but these sound higher and brighter when you use the **octave key** (see page 4).

Playing higher or lower is also known as playing a higher or lower **pitch**. The higher pitch notes need stronger air support and control, and can be more challenging for some players. These higher notes take steady practice to sound clean and confident.

Watch for the big change between the C and D notes. Keep your fingers close and ready.

Remember, each note comes with a fingering diagram showing you which keys to press.

- Black keys mean you should press those keys.
- White keys mean those keys stay untouched.

For this big change, keep your fingers close and ready.

Big Change!

G Major Scale (Up)

This is the low G major scale. We call it "Up" because the scale begins on the G note and moves higher in sound with each new note. This is also known as the **G major scale ascending**, which includes the notes G, A, B, C, D, E, and F# (F sharp). The word **sharp** means the note sounds slightly higher in pitch than the regular note, in this case F.

Watch for the big change between the C and D notes. Keep your fingers close and ready.

Remember, each note comes with a fingering diagram showing you which keys to press.

- Black keys mean you should press those keys.
- White keys mean those keys stay untouched.

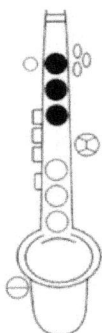

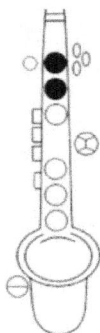

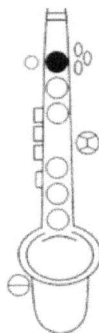

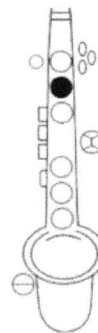

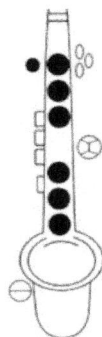

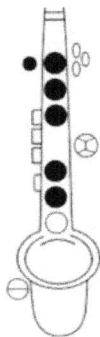

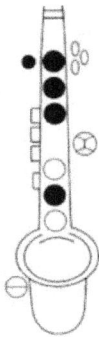

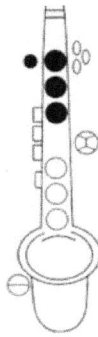

G Major Scale (Down)

Here is the G major scale going down. We call it "Down" because the scale begins on the higher G note and every new note goes lower in sound. This is also known as the **G major scale descending**

Remember, each note comes with a fingering diagram showing you which keys to press.

- Black keys mean you should press those keys.
- White keys mean those keys stay untouched.

F Major Scale (Low)

This is the F major scale (low). This scale makes your fingers really work. Use your right hand index finger on RH 1C (see page 4) to hit that B♭ note.

Take your time. Pause slightly between notes to keep your rhythm steady.

Remember, each note comes with a fingering diagram showing you which keys to press.

- Black keys mean you should press those keys.
- White keys mean those keys stay untouched.

F Major Scale (High)

This is the F major scale in the higher octave. When we press the octave key, we also say you've moved up a **register**. The higher register needs stronger air support and control, and can be more challenging for some players. These higher notes take steady practice to sound clean and confident.

The jumps between D, E, and high F can be hard to do at first. Practice the motion between these notes until you can make a smooth, even change in sound.

Remember, each note comes with a fingering diagram showing you which keys to press.

- Black keys mean you should press those keys.
- White keys mean those keys stay untouched.

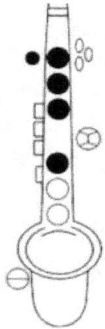

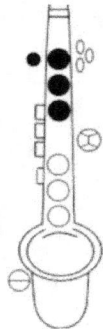

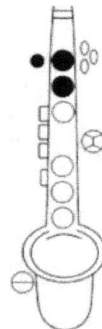

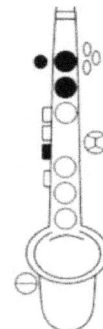

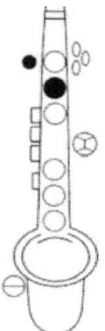

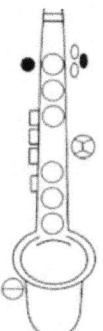

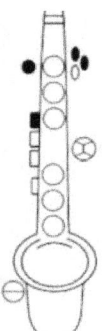

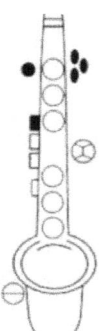

D Major Scale (Low)

Here is the D major scale beginning the alto saxophone's lowest D note. The D major scale includes the notes D, E, F#, G, A, B, and C#.

Remember, each note comes with a fingering diagram showing you which keys to press.

- Black keys mean you should press those keys.
- White keys mean those keys stay untouched.

For this big change, keep your fingers close and ready.

Big Change!

D Major Scale (High)

The D major scale in the higher register begins on D, one octave above the lower version. This register requires stronger air support and control and can be more challenging for some players. These higher notes take steady practice to sound clean and confident.

Remember, each note comes with a fingering diagram showing you which keys to press.

- Black keys mean you should press those keys.
- White keys mean those keys stay untouched.

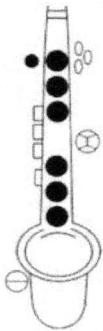

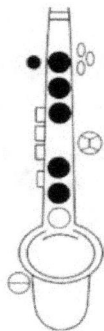

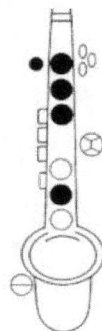

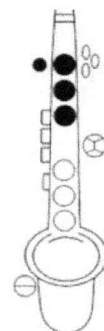

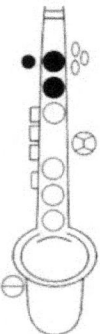

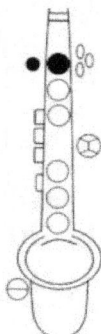

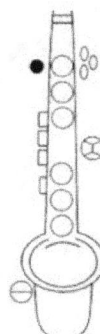

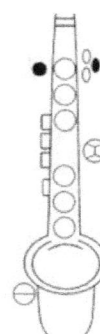

B♭ Major Scale (Low)

Here is the B♭ major scale (low). The starting B♭ note of this scale is the lowest note playable on an alto saxophone.

The B♭ major scale includes the notes B♭, C, D, E♭ , F, G, and A.

Remember, each note comes with a fingering diagram showing you which keys to press.

- Black keys mean you should press those keys.
- White keys mean those keys stay untouched.

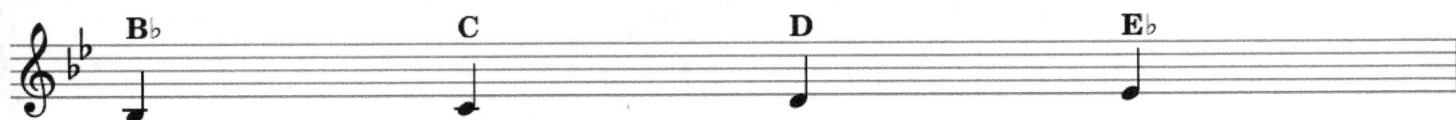

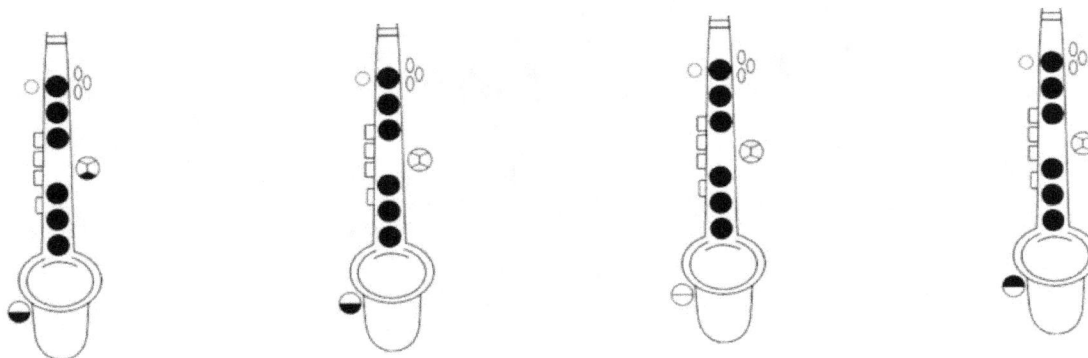

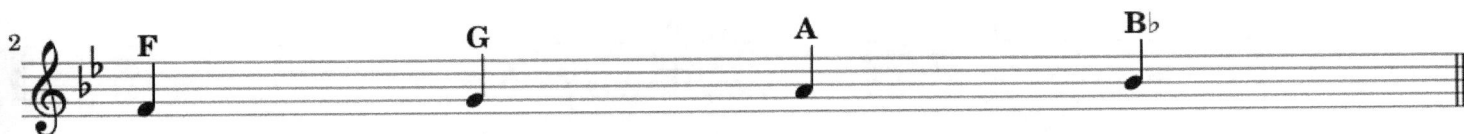

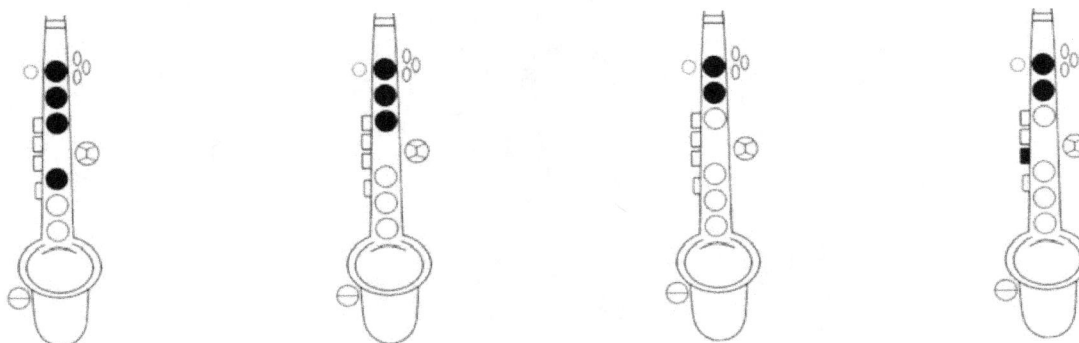

B♭ Major Scale (High)

This is the B♭ major scale in the higher register. The notes here are one octave higher than the B♭ major scale shown on the previous page.

Remember, each note comes with a fingering diagram showing you which keys to press.

- Black keys mean you should press those keys.
- White keys mean those keys stay untouched.

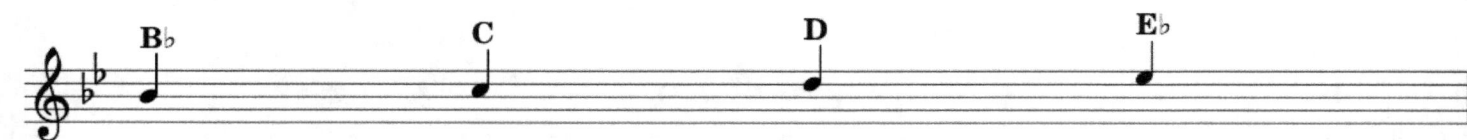

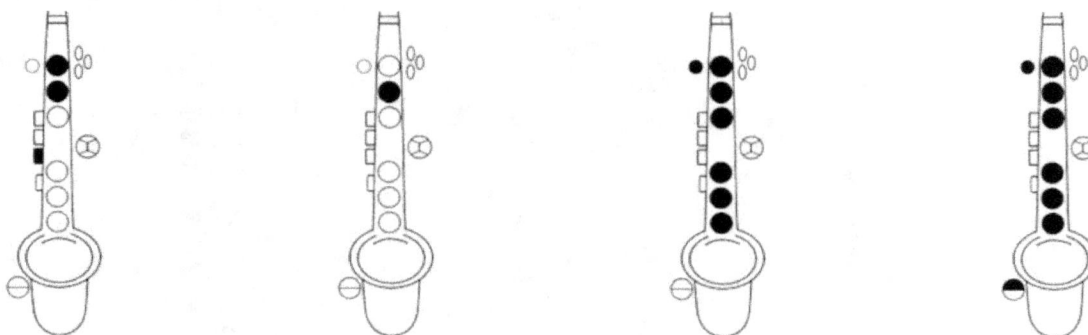

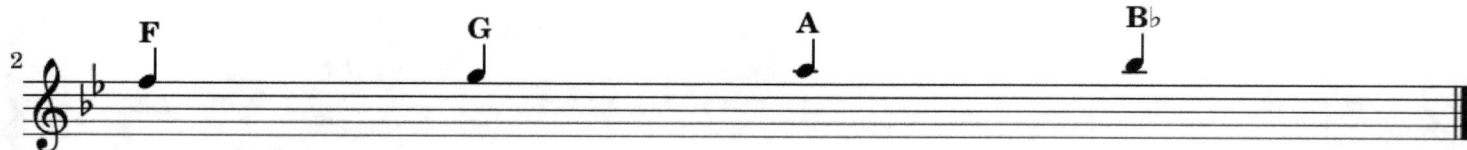

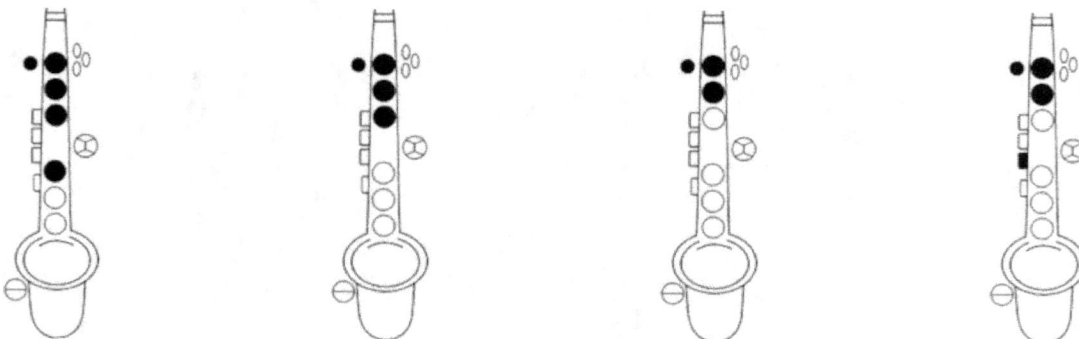

E♭ Major Scale (Low)

Here is the E♭ major scale in the lower register. The E♭ major scale includes the notes E♭, F, G, A♭, B♭, C, and D. Notice the position of your right-hand pinky when playing E♭.

The only difference in fingering between the low E♭ and the high E♭ is the use of your left thumb on the octave key.

Remember, each note comes with a fingering diagram showing you which keys to press.

- Black keys mean you should press those keys.
- White keys mean those keys stay untouched.

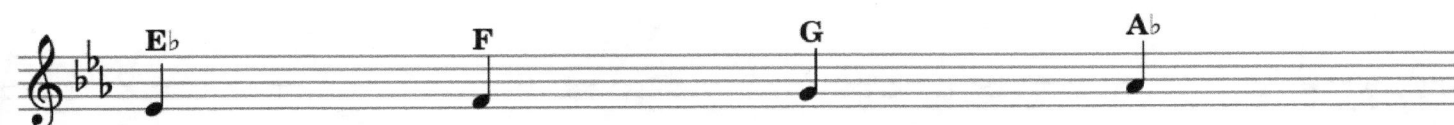

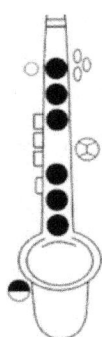

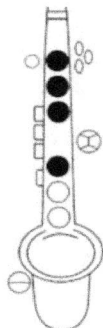

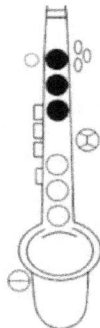

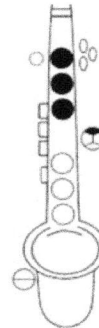

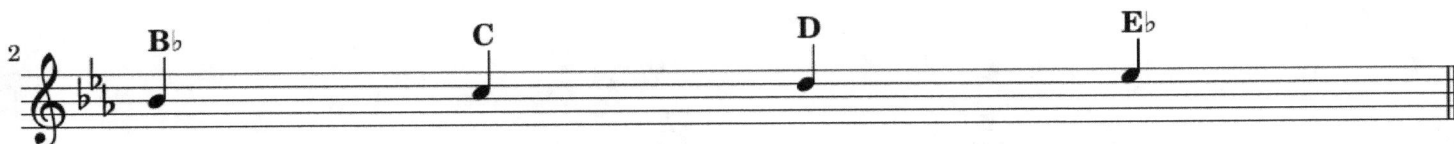

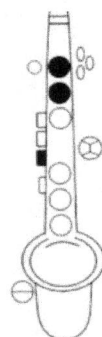

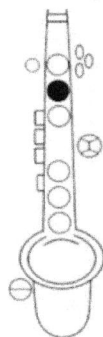

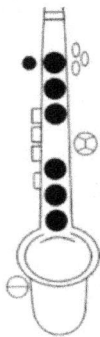

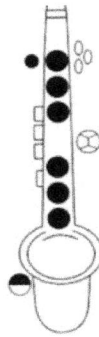

E♭ Major Scale (High)

This is the E♭ major scale played in the higher register. The higher register needs stronger air support and control, and can be more challenging for some players. These higher notes take steady practice to sound clean and confident.

The notes D and E♭ use the left-hand palm keys, which can be hard to use at first. Practice the motion between these notes until you can make a smooth, even change in sound.

Remember, each note comes with a fingering diagram showing you which keys to press.

- Black keys mean you should press those keys.
- White keys mean those keys stay untouched.

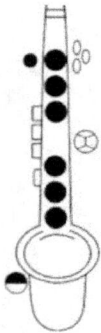

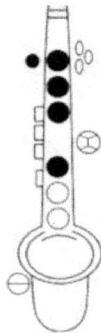

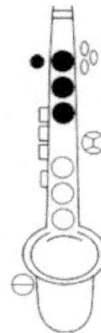

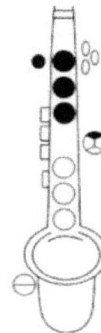

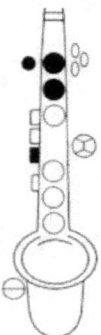

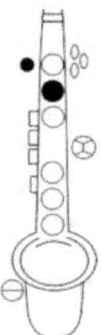

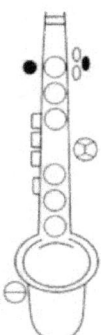

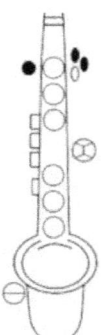

What is Your Embouchure?

em·bou·chure | \ ˌäm-bü-'shr

The embouchure is how a musician shapes and positions their lips, mouth, and facial muscles to control the sound and tone of a wind instrument, such as an alto saxophone. It's a delicate balance of coordination and pressure that transforms air into music, acting as the "control panel" for sound quality, pitch, and projection.

Your embouchure is how you use your lips, teeth, and mouth to play the saxophone, and it makes a big difference in how you sound. Let's talk about how to balance the pressure you use so your playing feels easier and your tone improves.

What Is Embouchure Pressure?

Think of your reed, lips, and teeth as a team working together to make music. If one part isn't doing its job, or doing too much, it can affect your sound.

Too much pressure: Your sound might become thin, sharp, or pinched.
Too little pressure: The tone could be airy, dull, or unfocused.

The goal is to find just the right amount of pressure so your reed vibrates freely, producing a clear, rich tone.

How do you know if something's off? Listen carefully.

Squeaks or chirps: Too much pressure or biting can stop the reed from vibrating evenly.
Breathy sound: Often happens when your lips don't seal well around the mouthpiece.
Flat tone: Sometimes caused by puffed cheeks or too little mouthpiece in the mouth.

Tips to Improve Your Embouchure

Bottom Lip: Roll it slightly over your bottom teeth to cushion the reed. Don't bite.

Top Teeth: Rest them gently on the top of the mouthpiece for stability.

Lip Shape: Form a firm but relaxed seal around the mouthpiece, like saying "Ooh."

20

Notes, Beats & How to Count Them

Here's a quick guide to the most common note types and how long each one lasts as you play.

Eighth (8th) notes
Each eighth note lasts for half a beat. Use steady air and move quickly to the next note.

When we see a plus sign: + we say 'and'

Quarter notes
A quarter note lasts 1 full beat. Use steady air and hold each note for one full beat. Each beat lasts the same amount of time.

Half notes
We play each half note for a count of 2 beats. Use steady air and hold each note for a full 2 beats. Each note lasts the same amount of time.

Whole notes
We count each whole note for 4 full beats. Use steady air and hold for 4 beats.

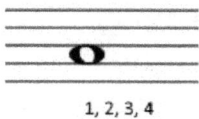

Dotted Quarter notes last for one and a half beats (that's 3 half beats).

How it works

A dot adds a little extra time—half the value of the note it's attached to.

Dotted Half notes each count for 3 beats. Use steady air and hold for 3 beats.

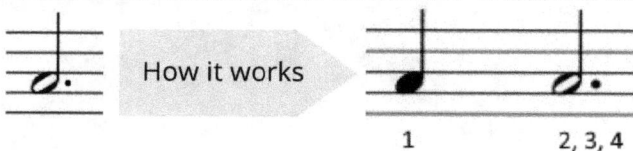

How it works

B Major Scale (Low)

Here is the B major scale in the lower register. The B major scale includes the notes B, C#, D#, E, F#, G#, and A#. Note the pinky positions in this scale for both left and right hands.

Remember, each note comes with a fingering diagram showing you which keys to press.

- Black keys mean you should press those keys.
- White keys mean those keys stay untouched.

B Major Scale (High)

Let's get into the B major scale played in the higher octave. The higher register needs stronger air support and control, and can be more challenging for some players. These higher notes take steady practice to sound clean and confident.

Remember, each note comes with a fingering diagram showing you which keys to press.

- Black keys mean you should press those keys.
- White keys mean those keys stay untouched.

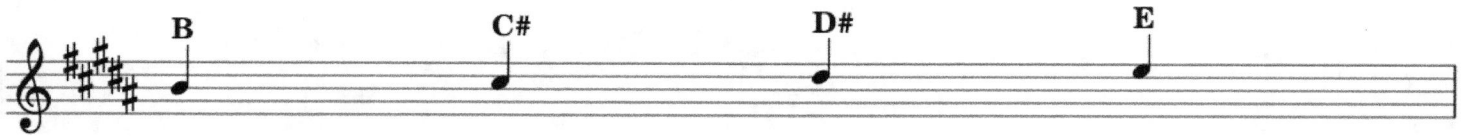

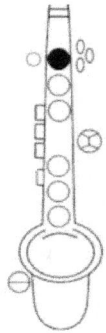

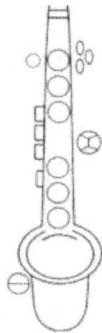

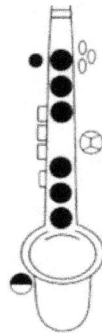

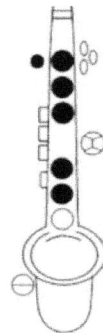

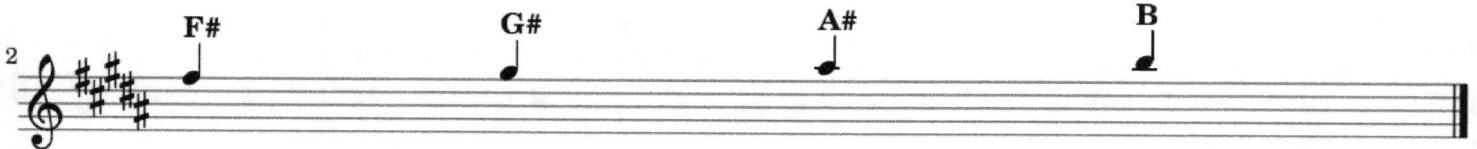

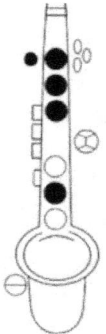

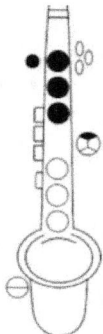

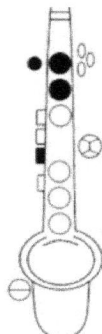

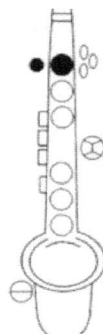

E Major Scale (Low)

Let's try the E major scale played in the lower register. The E major scale includes the notes E, F#, G#, A, B, C#, and D#. Note the pinky positions in this scale.

Remember, each note comes with a fingering diagram showing you which keys to press.

- Black keys mean you should press those keys.
- White keys mean those keys stay untouched.

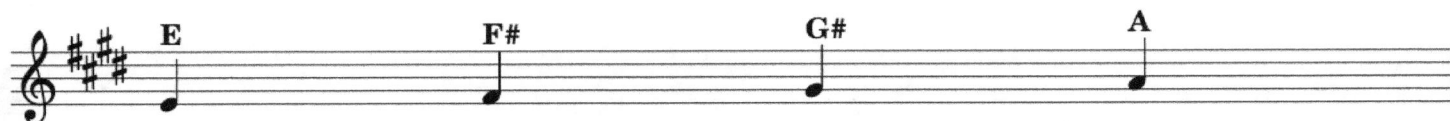

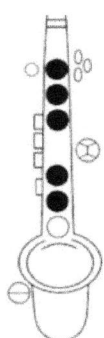

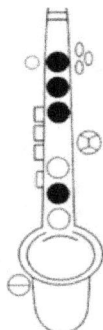

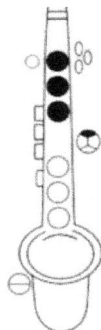

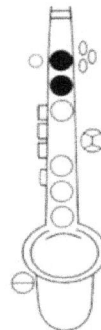

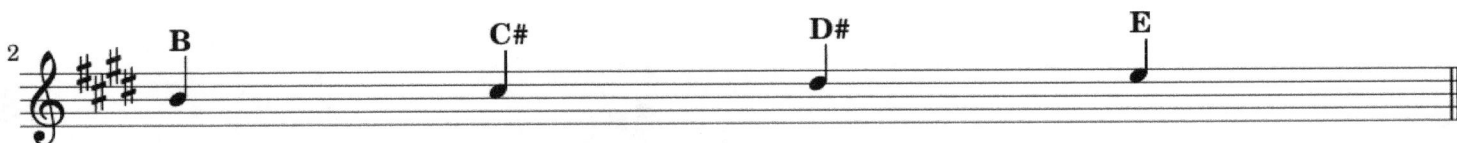

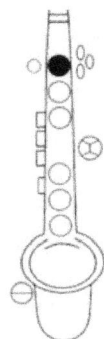

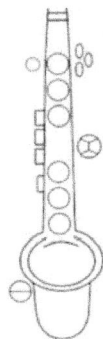

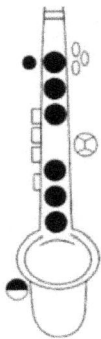

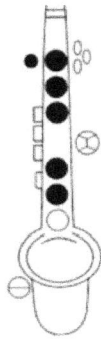

E Major Scale (High)

This is the E major scale in a higher register. The higher register needs stronger air support and control, and can be more challenging for some players. These higher notes take steady practice to sound clean and confident.

The notes D# and high E use the left-hand palm keys, which can be hard to use at first. Practice the motion between these notes until you can make a steady change in sound.

Remember, each note comes with a fingering diagram showing you which keys to press.

- Black keys mean you should press those keys.
- White keys mean those keys stay untouched.

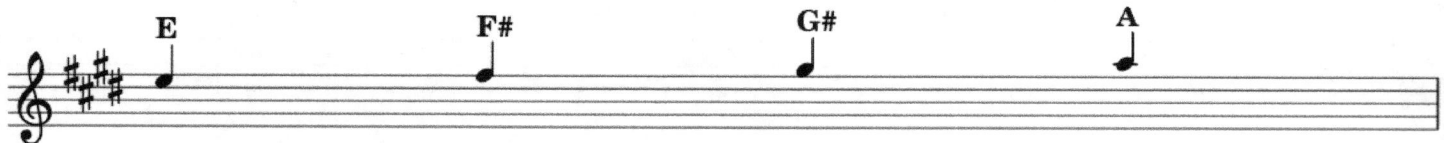

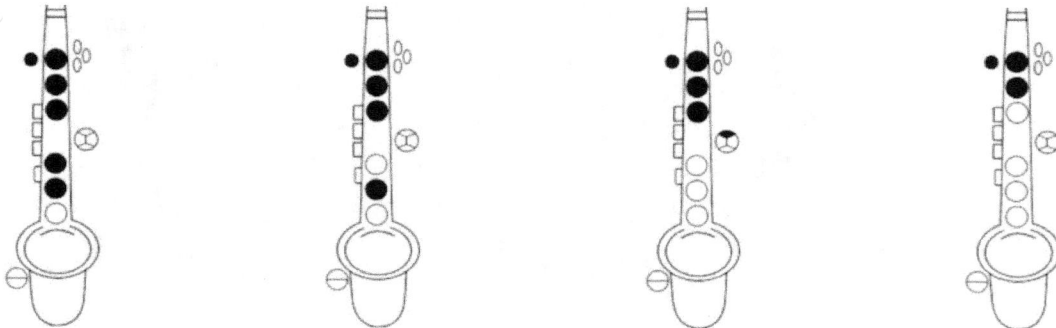

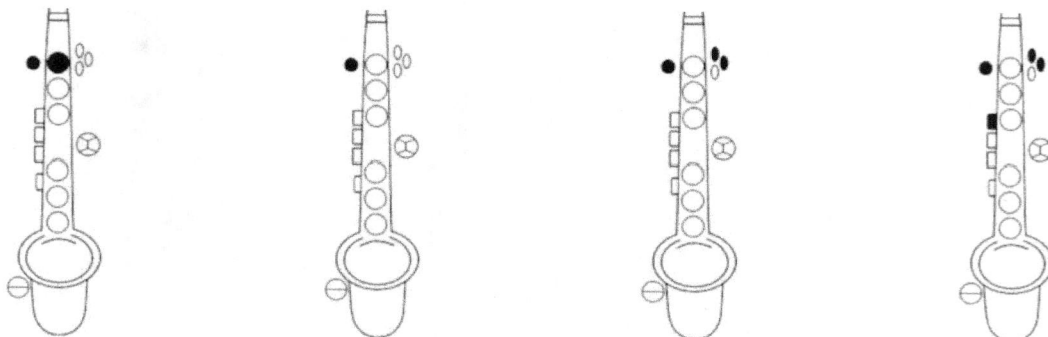

D♭ Major Scale (Low)

Here is the D♭ major scale in the lower register. The D♭ major scale includes the notes D♭, E♭, F, G♭, A♭, B♭, and C.

Remember, each note comes with a fingering diagram showing you which keys to press.

- Black keys mean you should press those keys.
- White keys mean those keys stay untouched.

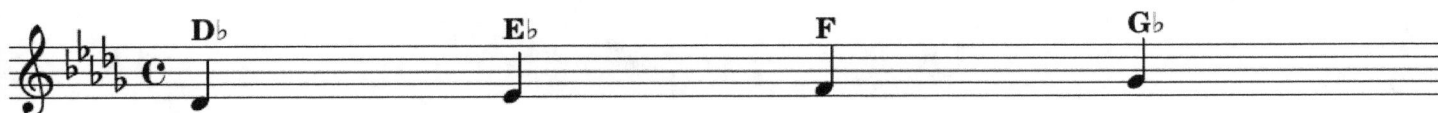

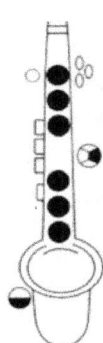

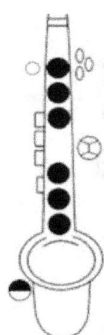

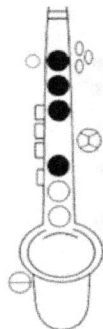

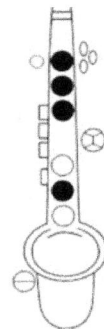

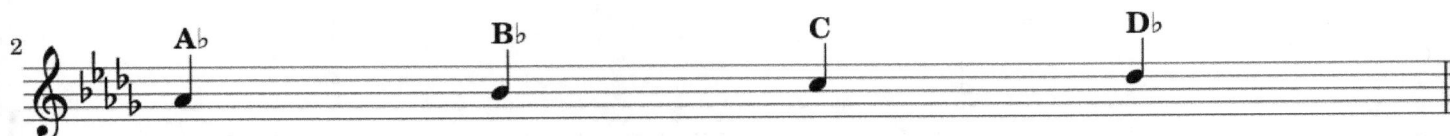

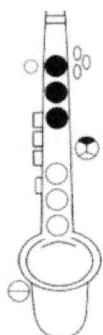

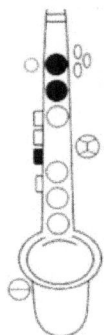

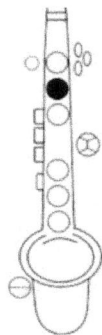

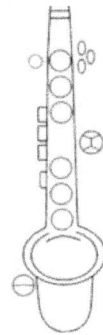

D♭ Major Scale (High)

This is the D♭ major scale in the higher octave. The higher register needs stronger air support and control, and can be more challenging for some players. These higher notes take steady practice to sound clean and confident.

Remember, each note comes with a fingering diagram showing you which keys to press.

- Black keys mean you should press those keys.
- White keys mean those keys stay untouched.

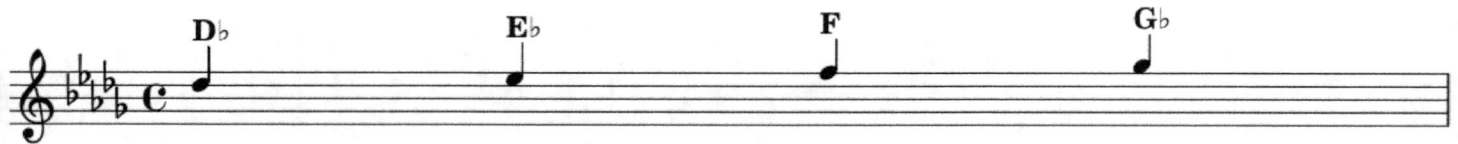

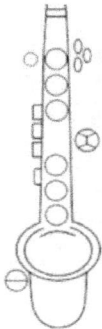

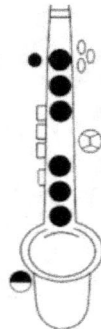

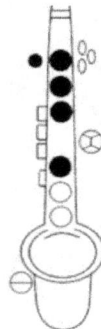

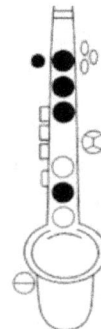

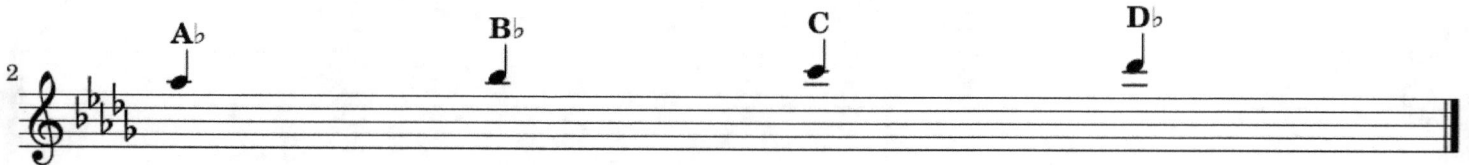

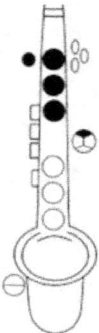

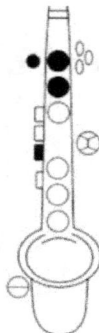

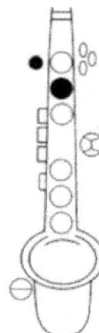

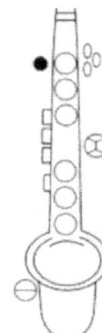

A♭ Major Scale (Up)

This is the A♭ major scale ascending. The A♭ major scale includes the notes A♭, B♭, C, D♭, E♭, F, and G. For this scale, note the pinky positions on the left and right hands.

Remember, each note comes with a fingering diagram showing you which keys to press.

- Black keys mean you should press those keys.
- White keys mean those keys stay untouched.

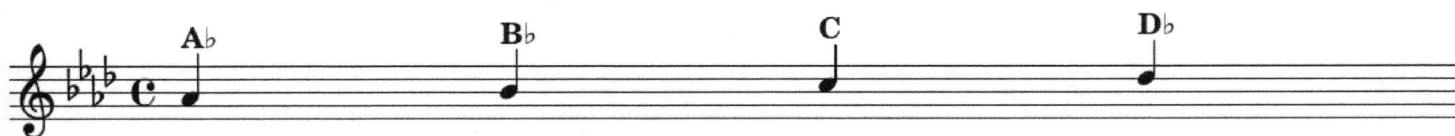

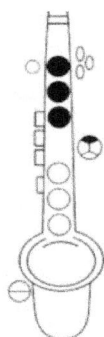

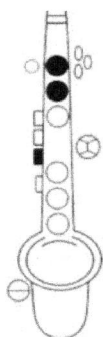

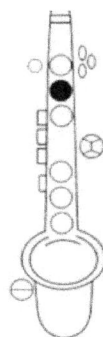

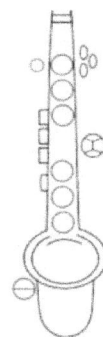

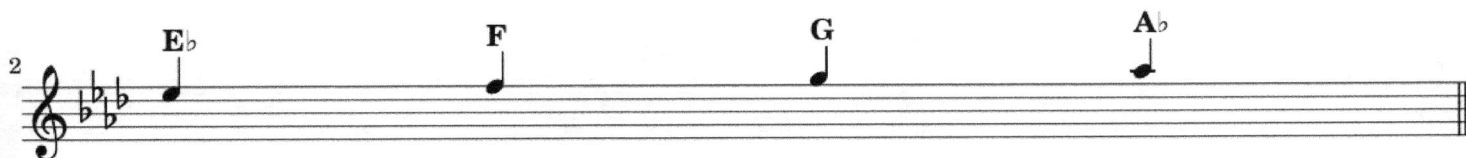

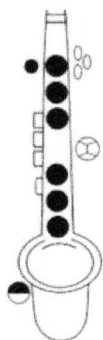

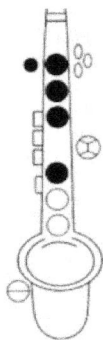

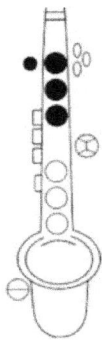

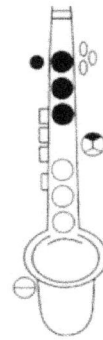

A♭ Major Scale (Down)

Here is the A♭ major scale descending. This scale gives your fingers a workout.

Remember, each note comes with a fingering diagram showing you which keys to press.

- Black keys mean you should press those keys.
- White keys mean those keys stay untouched.

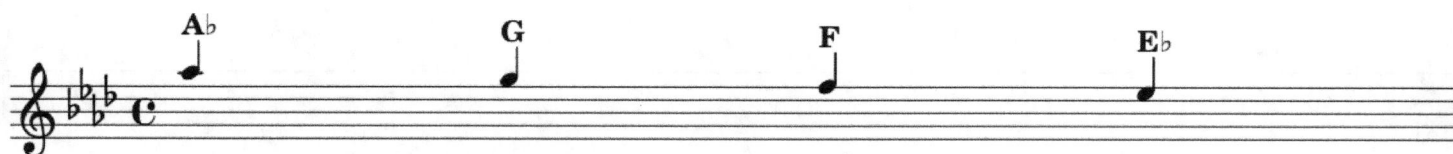

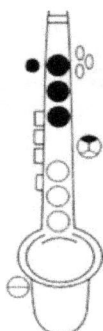

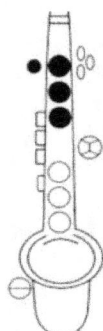

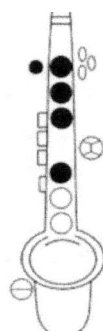

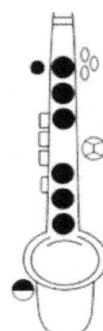

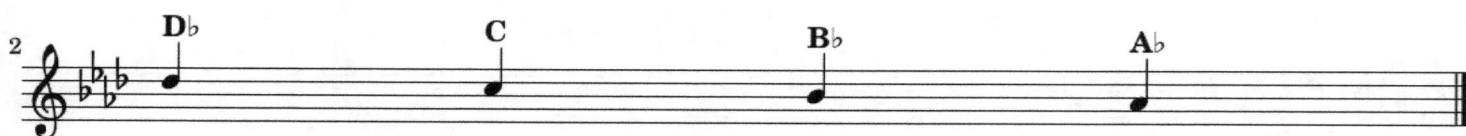

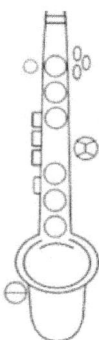

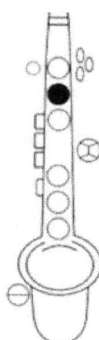

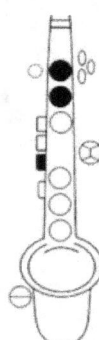

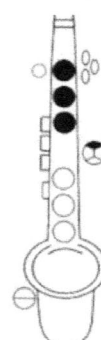

A Major Scale (Up)

This is the A major scale ascending. The A major scale includes the notes A, B, C#, D, E, F#, and G#. Note the position of the left hand pinky when playing the G#.

Remember, each note comes with a fingering diagram showing you which keys to press.

- Black keys mean you should press those keys.
- White keys mean those keys stay untouched.

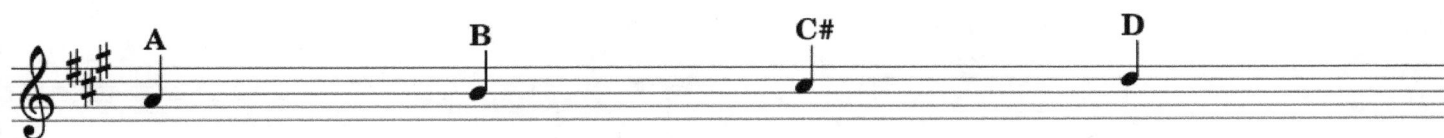

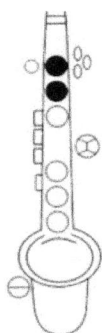

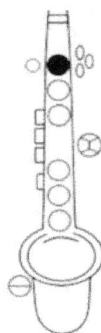

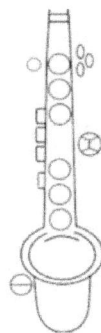

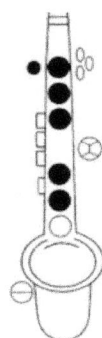

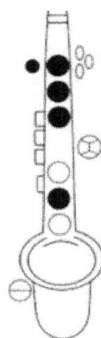

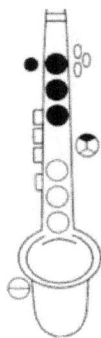

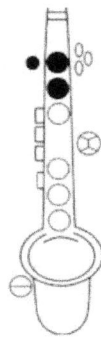

A Major Scale (Down)

Here is the A major scale descending. This scale gives your fingers a workout.

Remember, each note comes with a fingering diagram showing you which keys to press.

- Black keys mean you should press those keys.
- White keys mean those keys stay untouched.

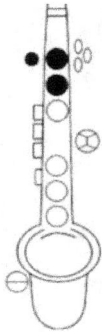

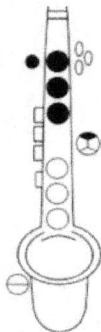

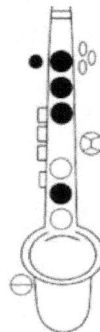

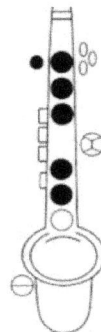

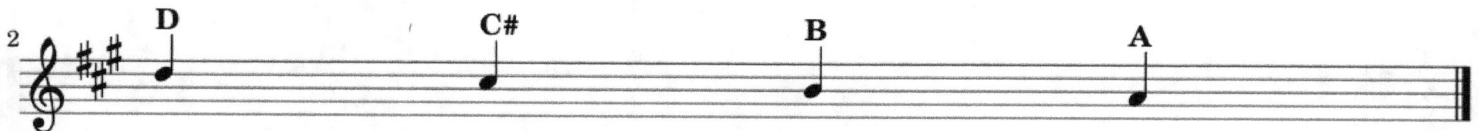

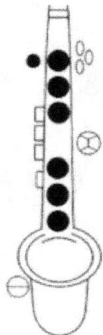

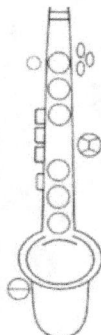

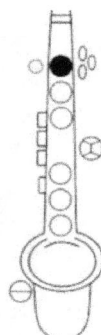

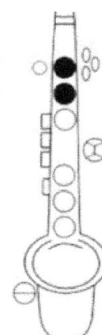

G♭ Major Scale (Up)

This is the G♭ major scale ascending. The G♭ major scale includes the notes G♭, A♭, B♭, C♭ (C♭ is the same as B), D♭, E♭, and F.

In music, some notes can have two names even though they sound exactly the same. This is called being **enharmonic.** C♭ (C flat) and B are one of these pairs.

When you see C♭, it means *play one half step lower than C.* When you move one half step lower from C, you land on B. So even though they look different on paper, C♭ and B sound the same when you play them.

Remember, each note comes with a fingering diagram showing you which keys to press.

- Black keys mean you should press those keys.
- White keys mean those keys stay untouched.

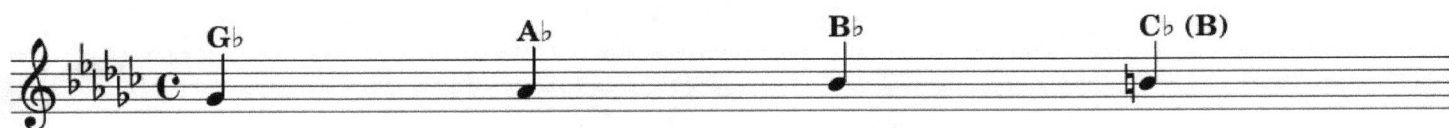

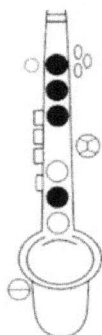

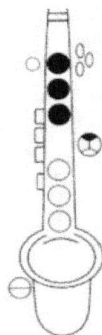

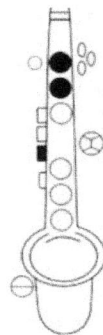

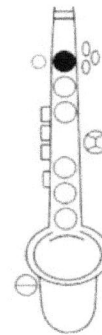

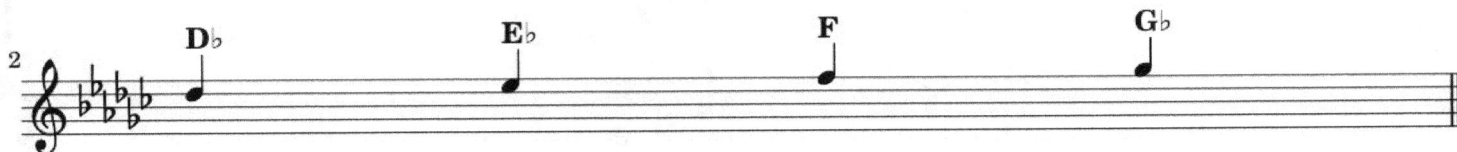

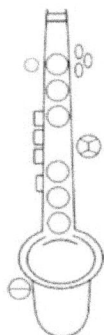

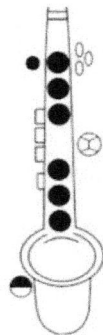

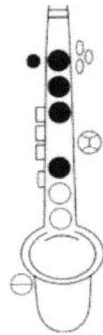

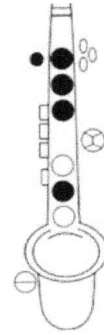

G♭ Major Scale (Down)

This is the G♭ major scale descending. Note that C♭ is enharmonic with B (see previous page), so they are fingered exactly the same way.

Remember, each note comes with a fingering diagram showing you which keys to press.

- Black keys mean you should press those keys.
- White keys mean those keys stay untouched.

The Warm-Up Song

Martin Freres (2025)

Here is a simple warm-up song played in the lower register using higher and lower notes. Use this warm-up any time before playing your scales or songs to give your lips, lungs, and fingers a workout.

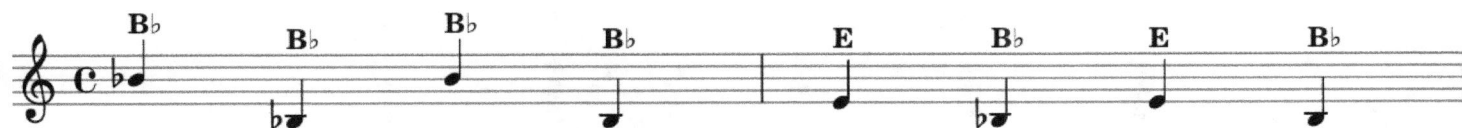

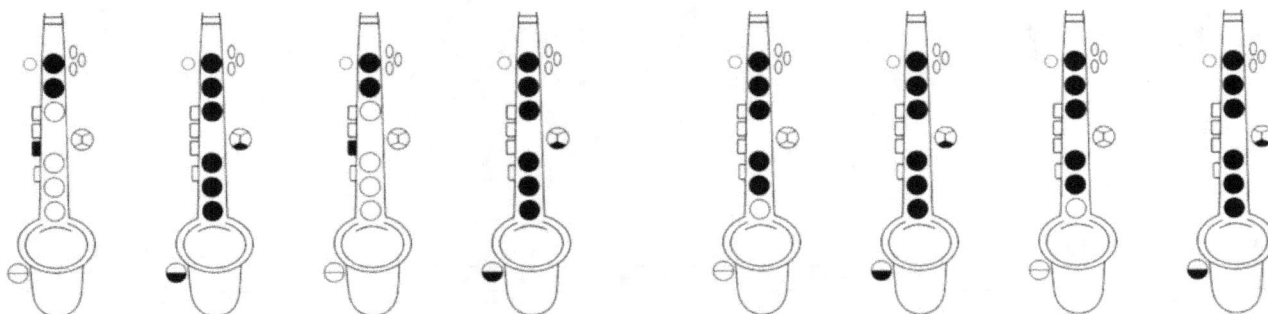

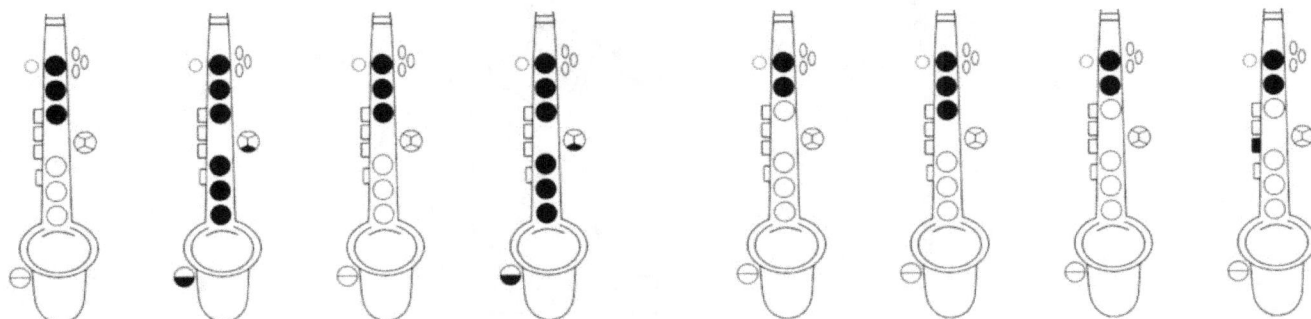

How to Use the QR Code

Scan the QR code with your phone or tablet camera to hear the song. Listen and play what you hear. QR codes allow you to hear how the notes and rhythm sound together.

Scan the
QR Code

to Listen to
the song!

Mary Had a Little Lamb

Lowell Mason (1831)

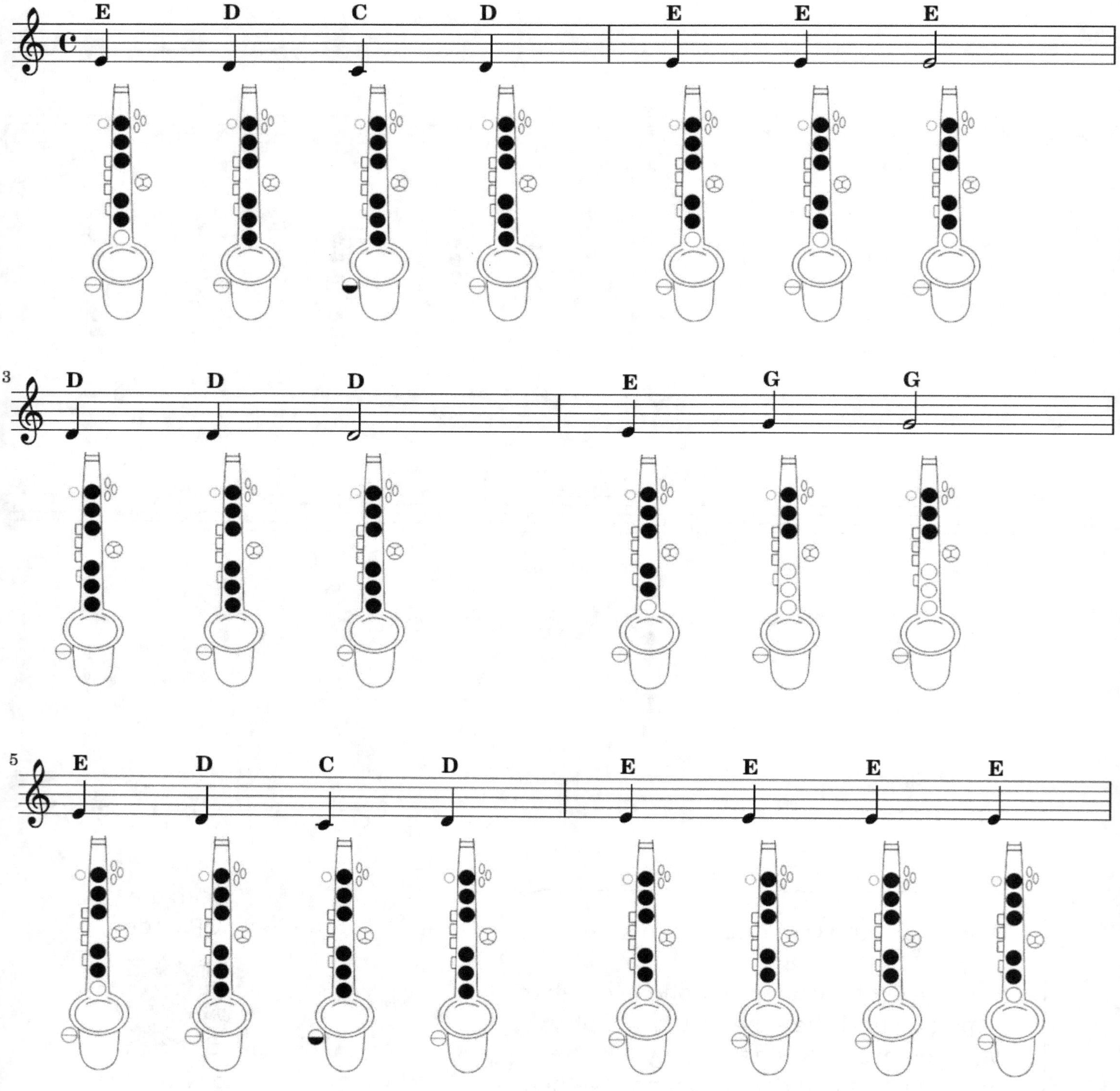

The Legend of Mary and Her Lamb

As the legend goes, this song was inspired by an actual event involving a girl named Mary Elizabeth Sawyer (1806–1889), who lived in Sterling, Massachusetts. According to Mary's writings, when she was a young girl, she nursed a sickly lamb back to health, and the lamb became attached to her. One day, the lamb followed Mary to school, creating a scene that amused her classmates and teacher.

Today, the Redstone Schoolhouse, where Mary's lamb supposedly followed her, is preserved as a historical site in Sudbury, Massachusetts, and continues to commemorate the tale.

Scan the
QR Code

to Listen to
the song!

Twinkle Twinkle Little Star

Traditional (1806)

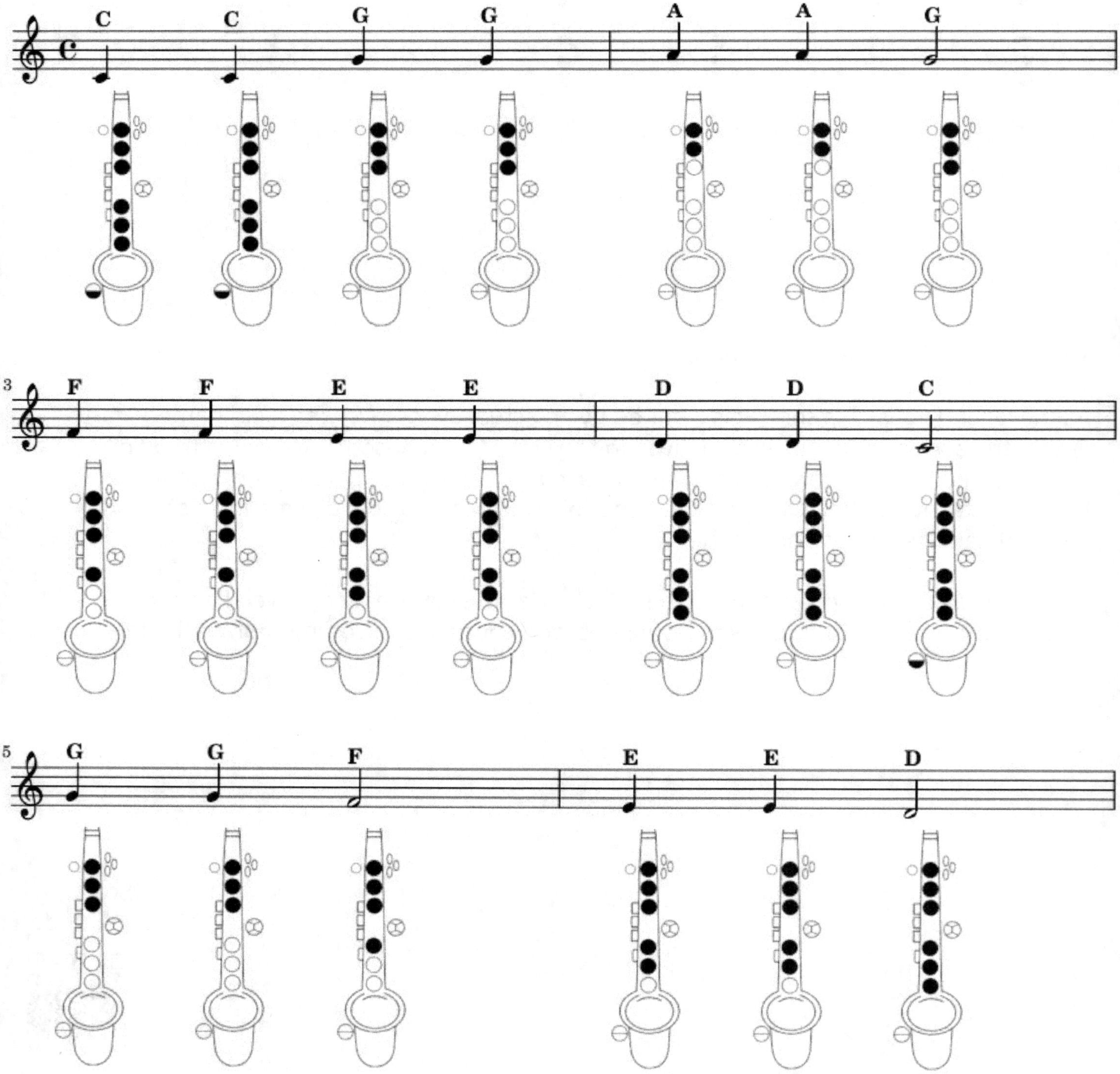

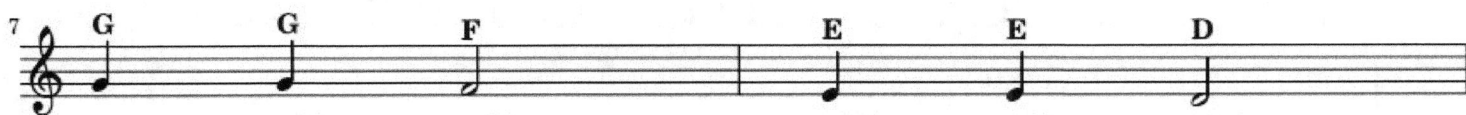

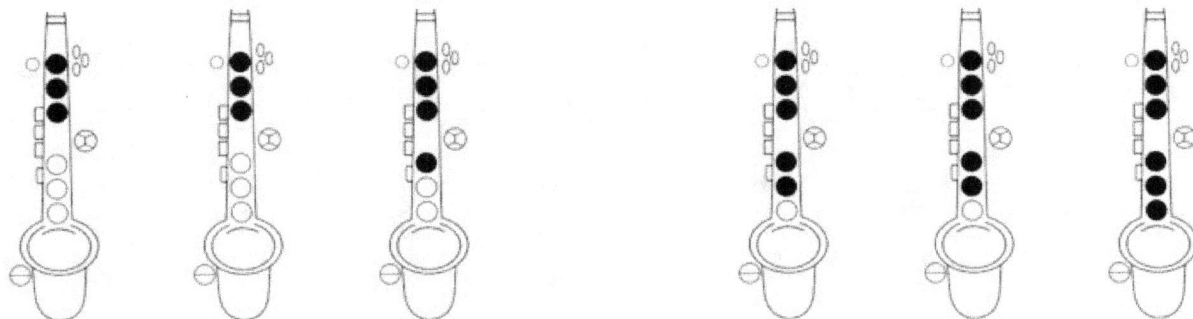

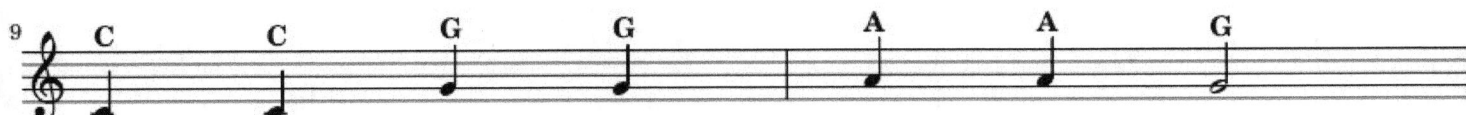

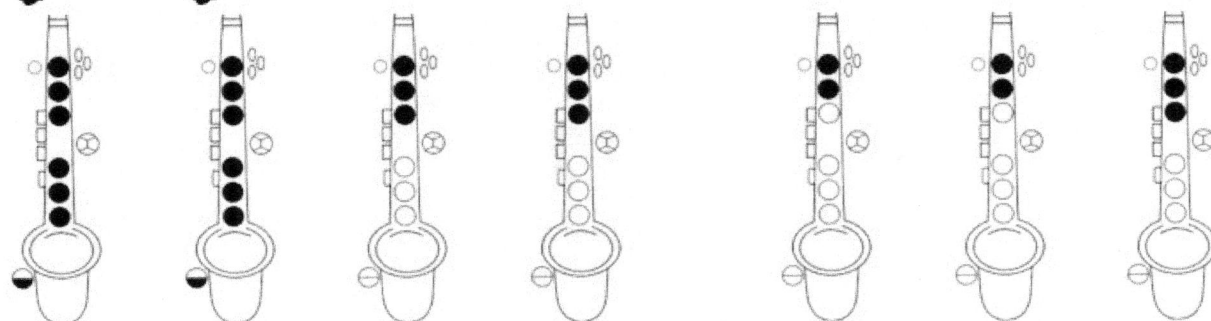

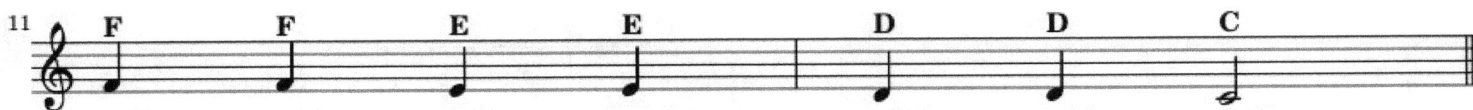

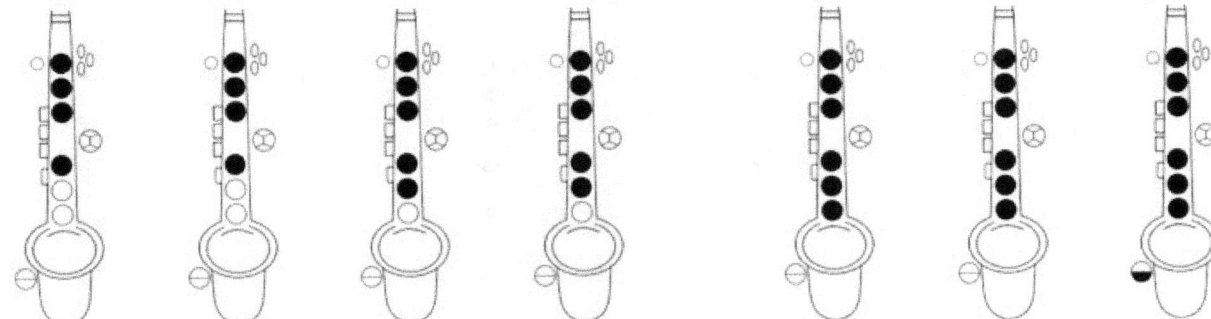

Scan the QR Code

to Listen to the song!

Frère Jacques (Brother John)

Traditional French (18th Century)

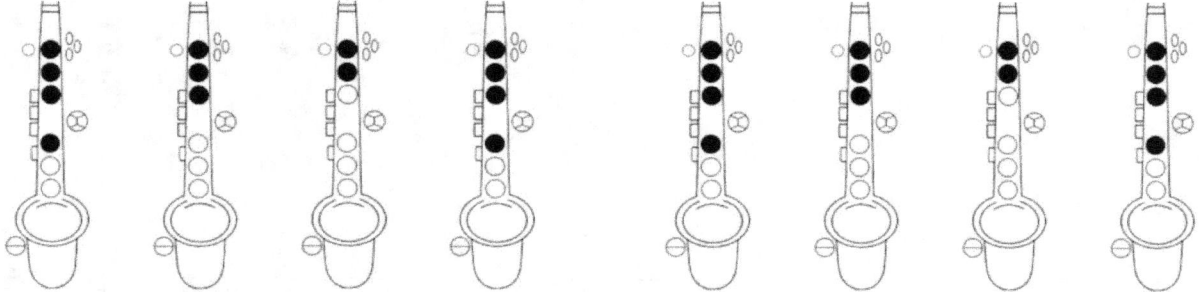

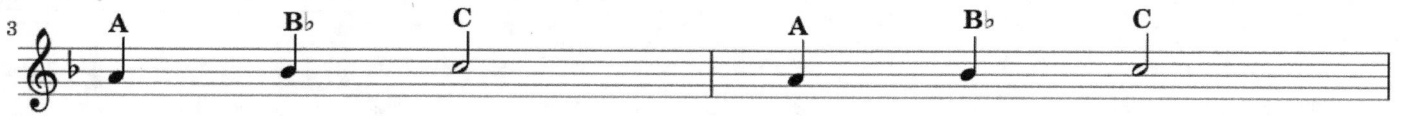

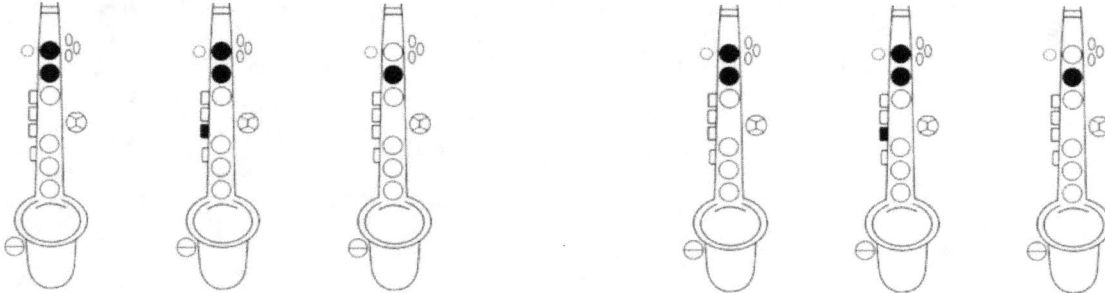

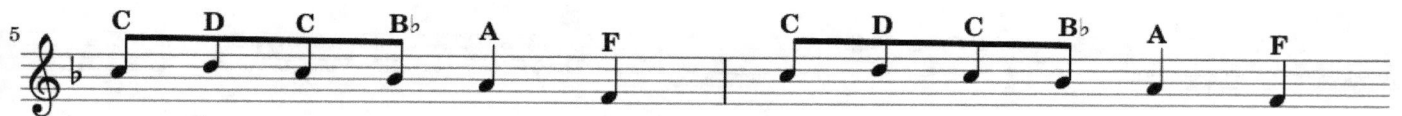

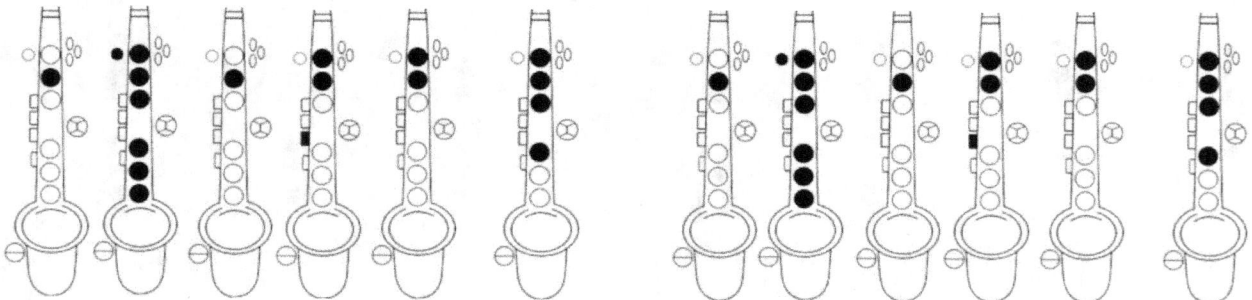

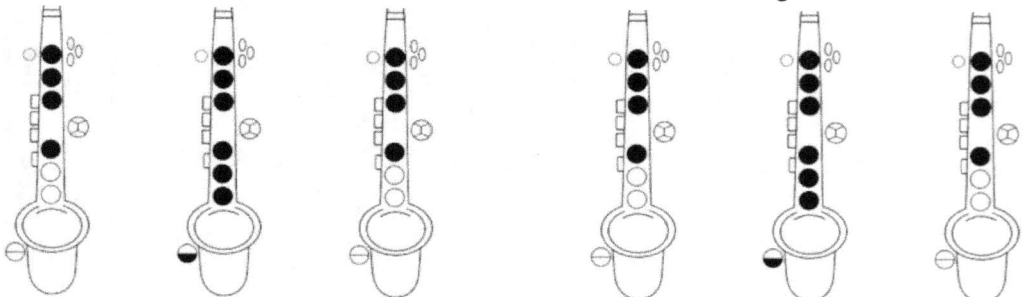

Scan the QR Code to Listen to the song!

Pop Goes the Weasel

Traditional English (c1850)

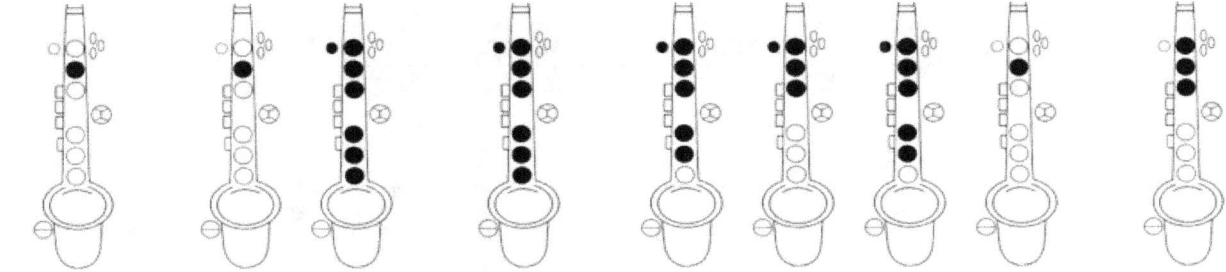

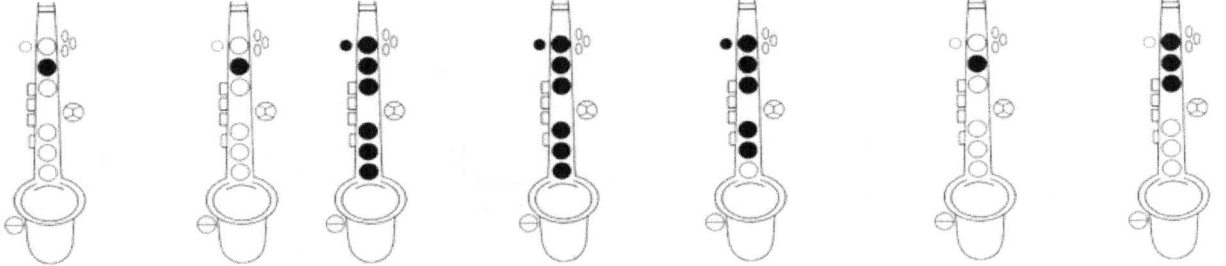

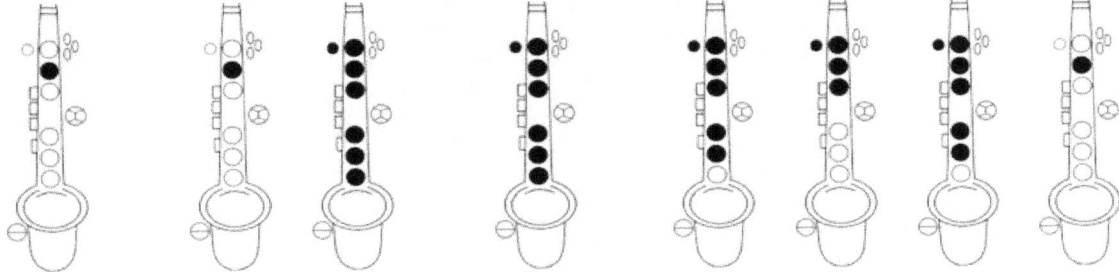

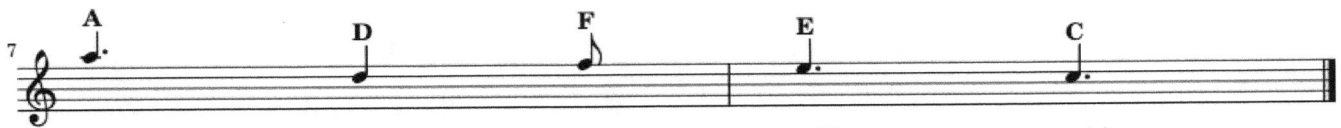

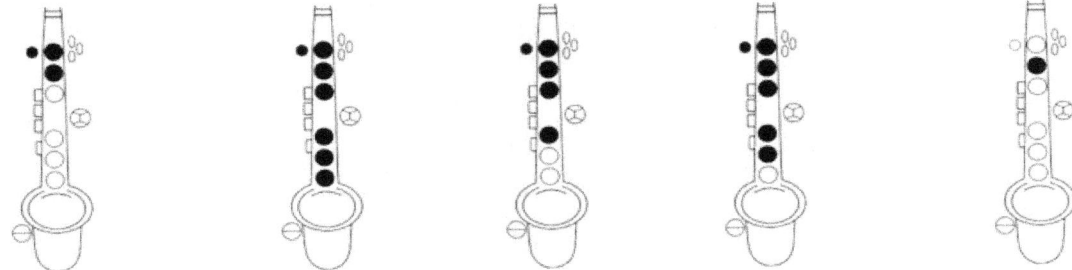

Scan the
QR Code

to Listen to
the song!

Ring Around the Rosie

Traditional English (19th Century)

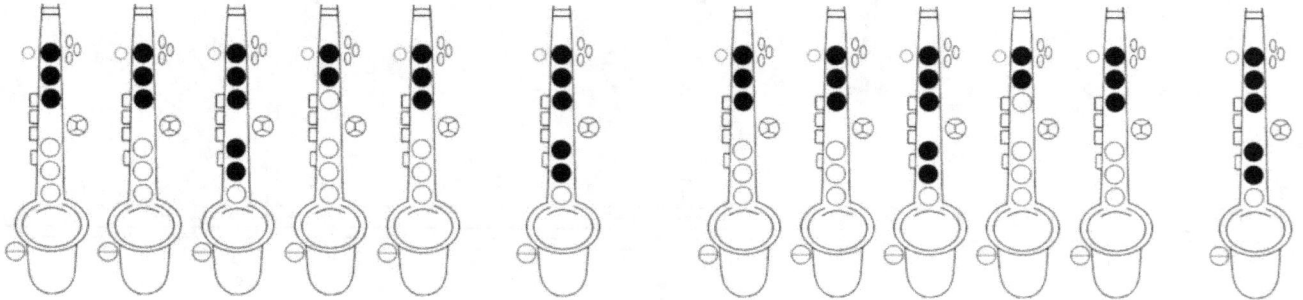

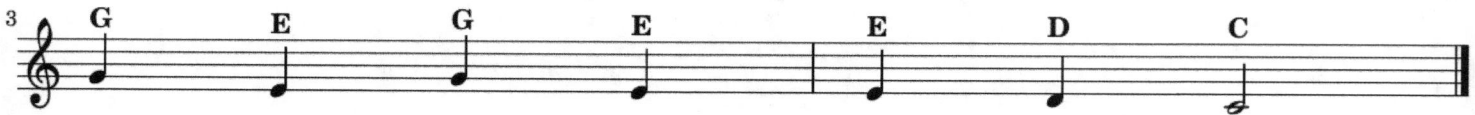

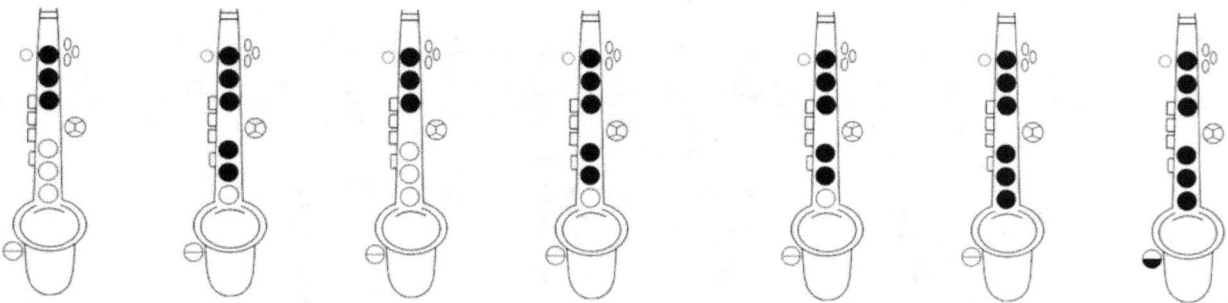

Scan the
QR Code

to Listen to
the song!

Row Row Row Your Boat

Traditional American (19th Century)

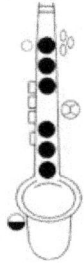

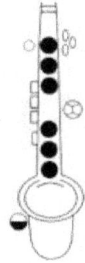

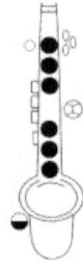

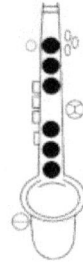

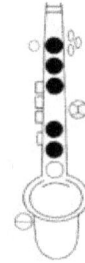

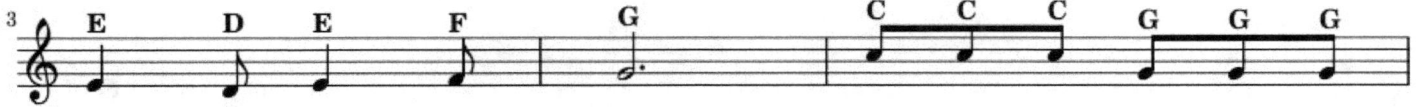

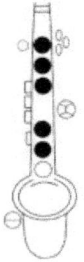

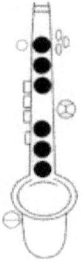

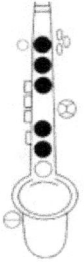

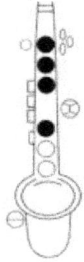

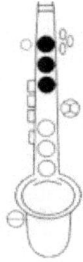

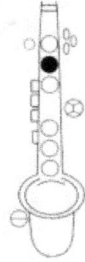

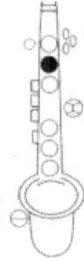

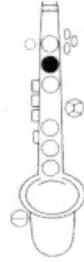

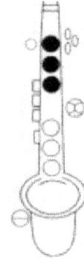

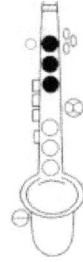

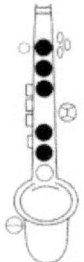

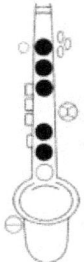

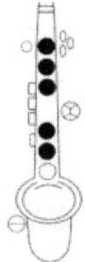

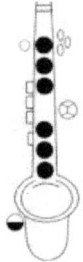

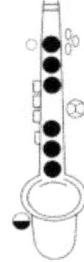

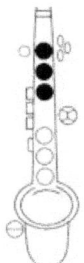

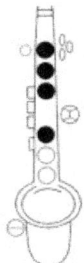

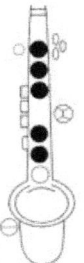

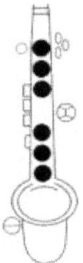

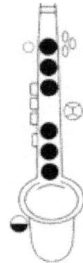

Scan the QR Code

to Listen to the song!

This Old Man

Traditional English (19th Century)

Scan the
QR Code

to Listen to
the song!

London Bridge is Falling Down

Traditional English (18th Century)

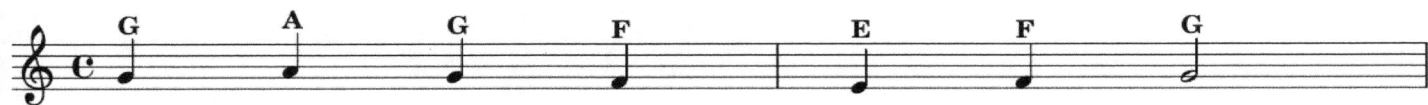

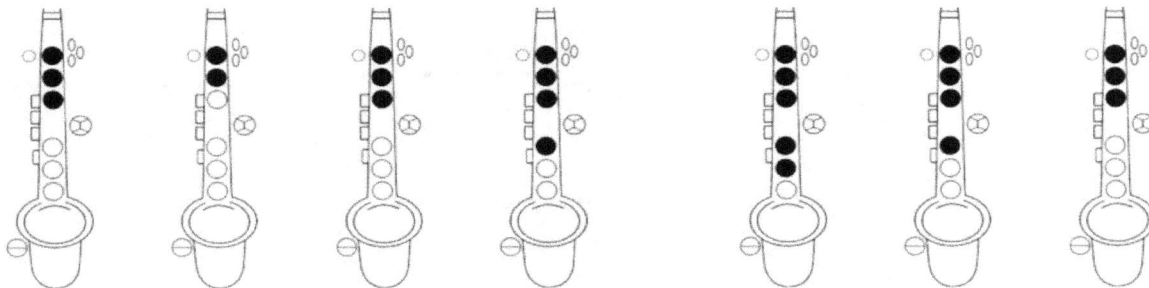

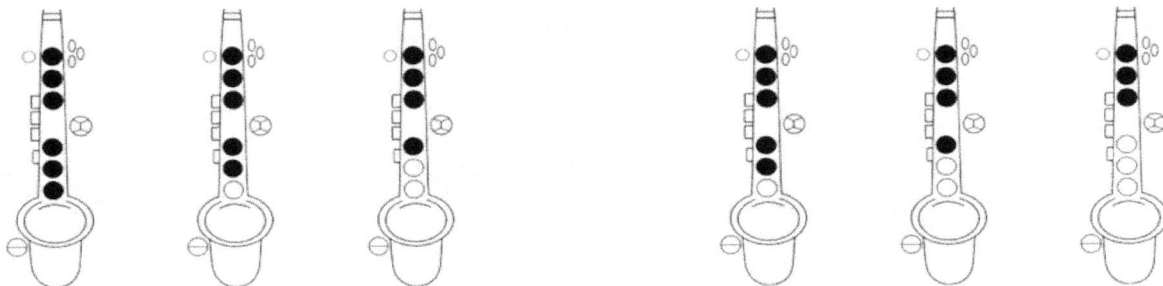

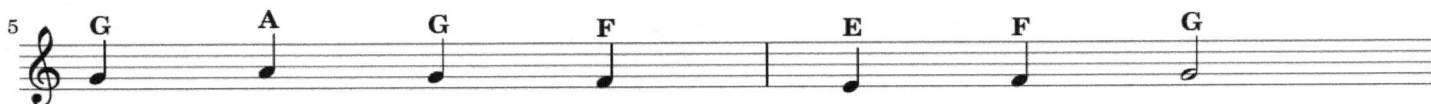

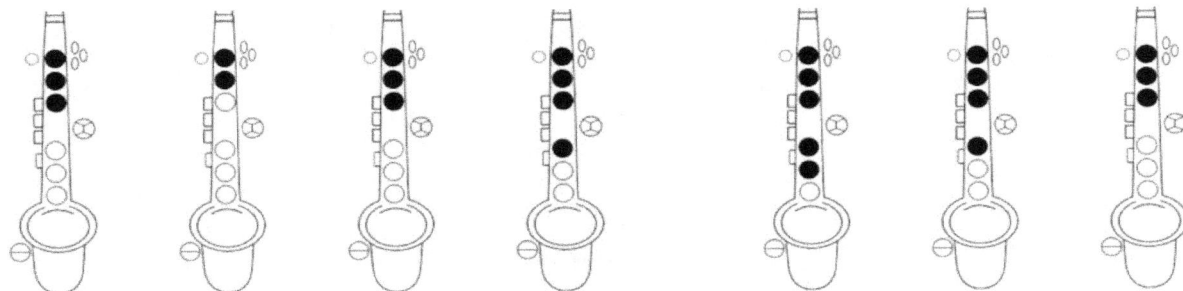

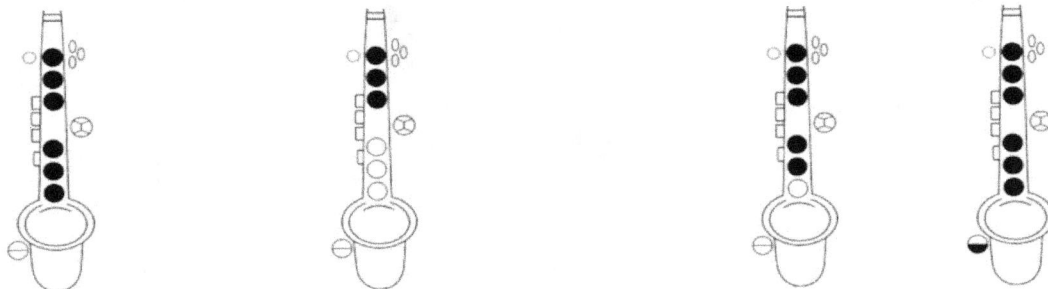

Scan the QR Code

to Listen to the song!

It's a Jazzy Day!

Martin Freres (2025)

It's a Jazzy Day!

This one is a tune that
hits the low notes and
jumps an octave higher.

IT'S A JAZZY DAY

Scan the
QR Code

to Listen to
the song!

Camptown Races

Stephen Foster (1850)

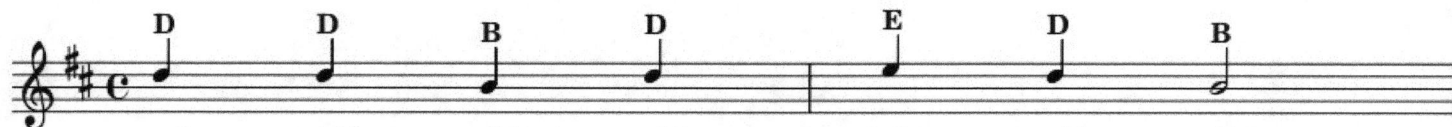

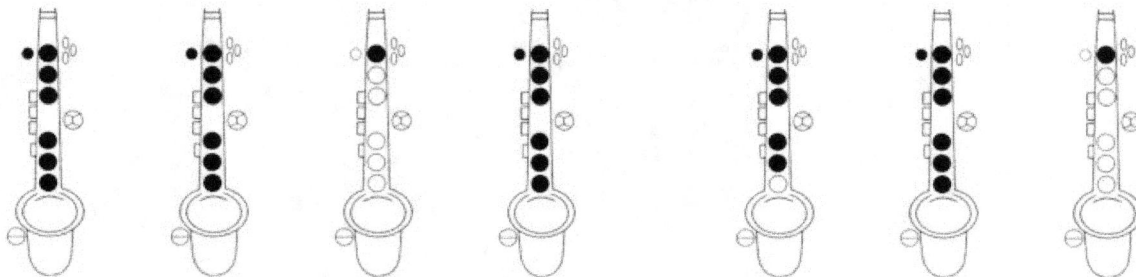

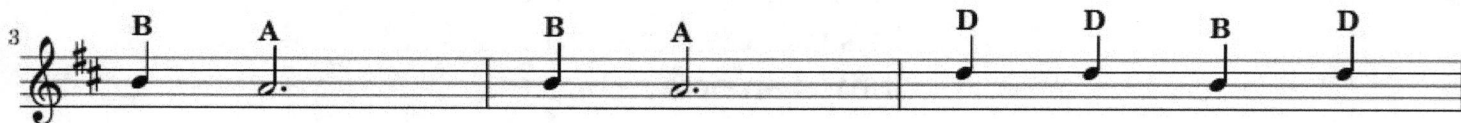

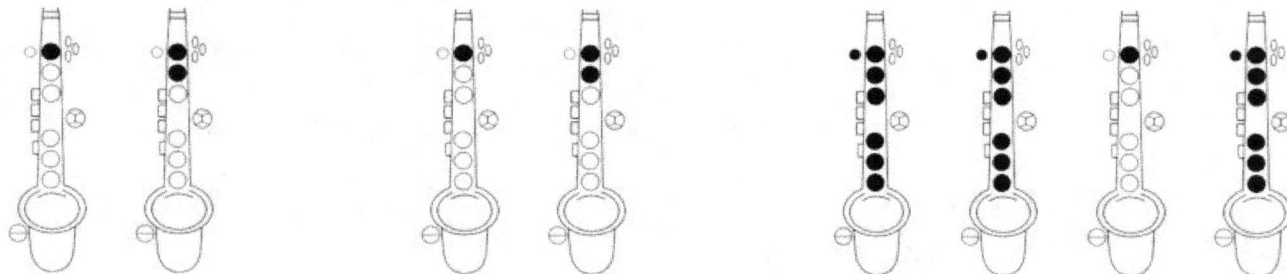

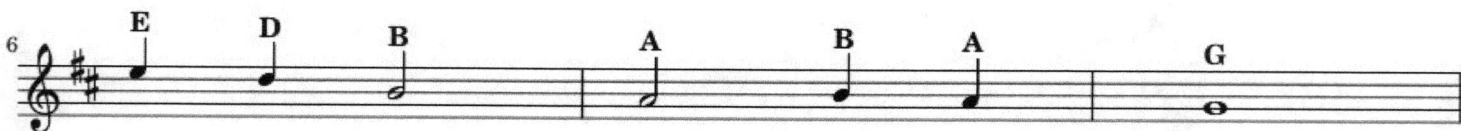

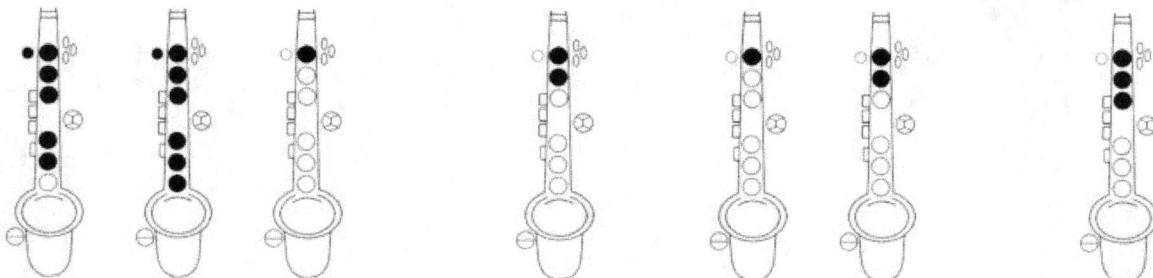

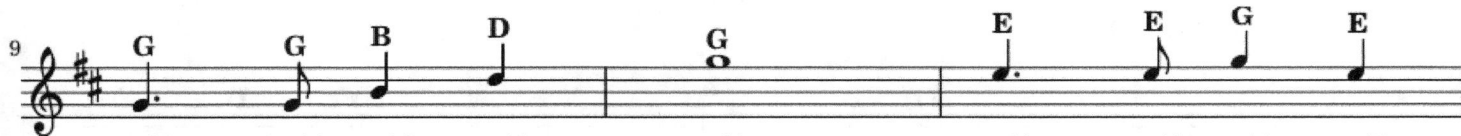

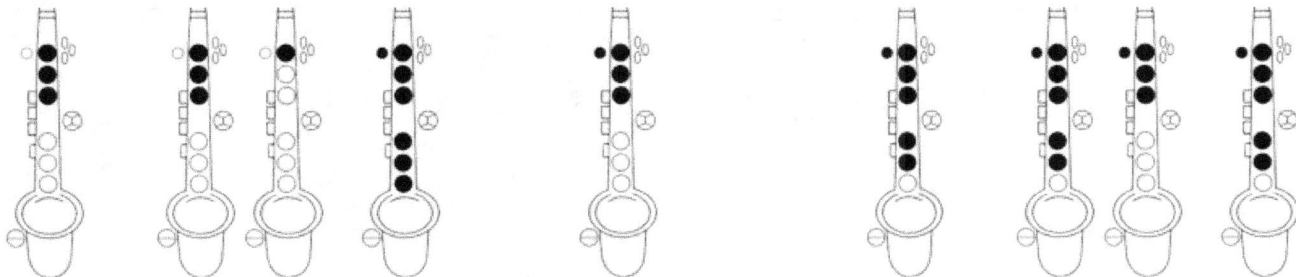

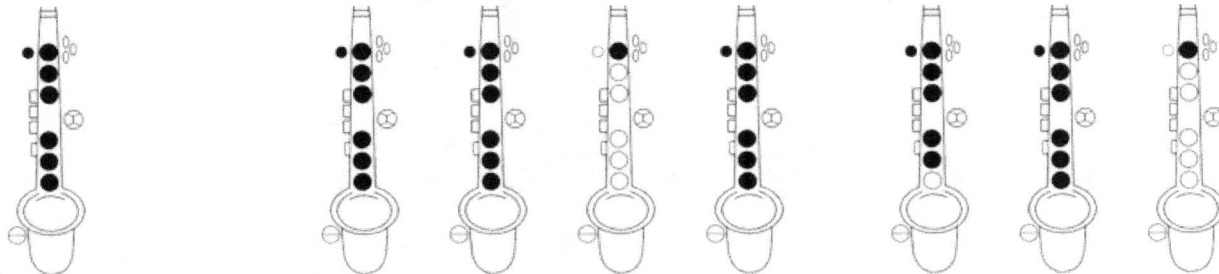

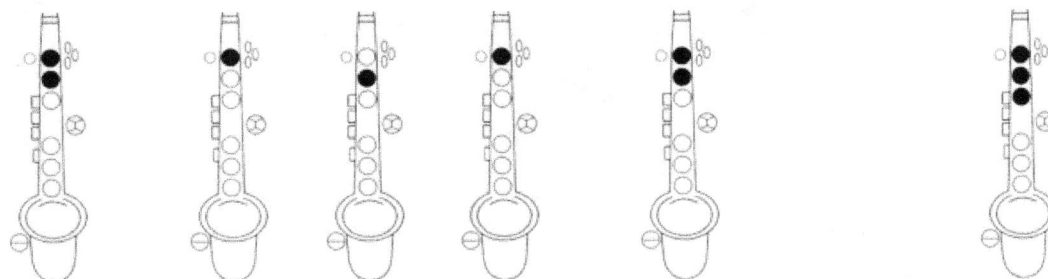

Stephen C. Foster (1826–1864)

Known as the "Father of American Music," Stephen Foster wrote songs that became part of America's cultural history. Born in Pennsylvania on July 4, 1826, he composed beloved tunes such as *Camptown Races, Oh! Susanna,* and *That's What's the Matter*, all featured in this book. His music remains timeless, simple, and memorable, ideal for learning melody, rhythm, and phrasing.

Scan the QR Code

to Listen to the song!

Oh! Susanna

Stephen Foster (1848)

Scan the
QR Code

to Listen to
the song!

That's What's the Matter

Stephen Foster (1862)

Scan the QR Code to Listen to the song!

Ode to Joy

Ludwig van Beethoven (1824)

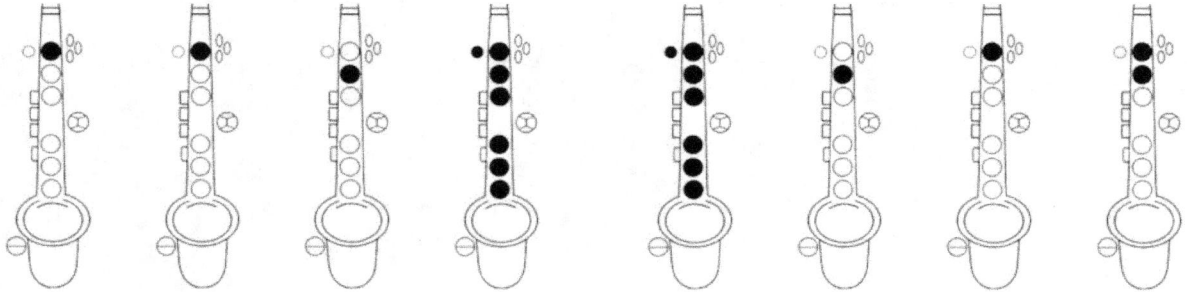

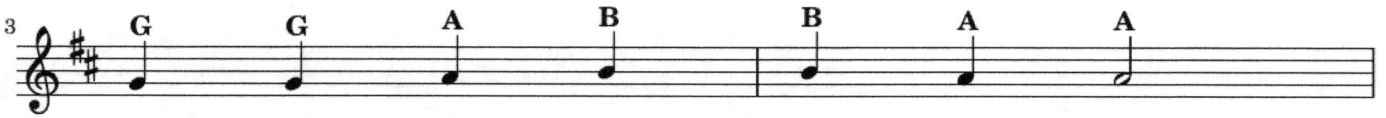

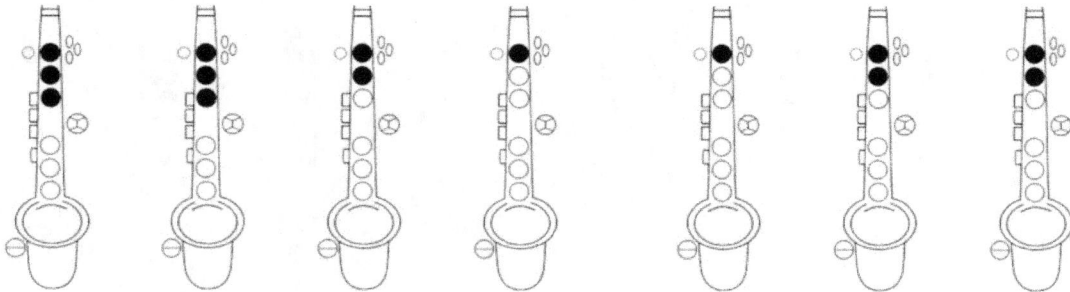

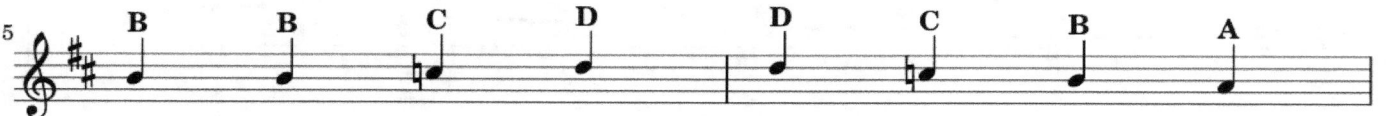

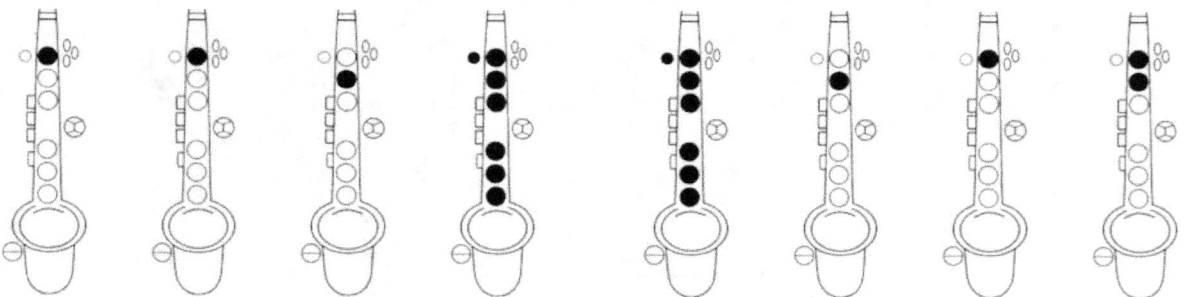

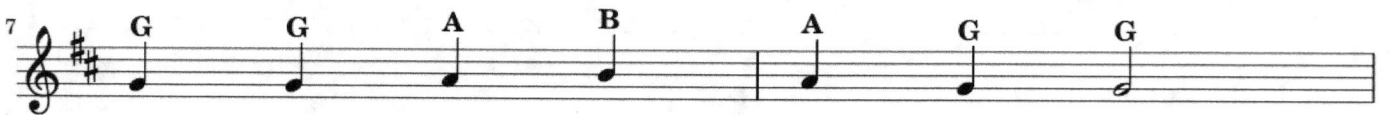

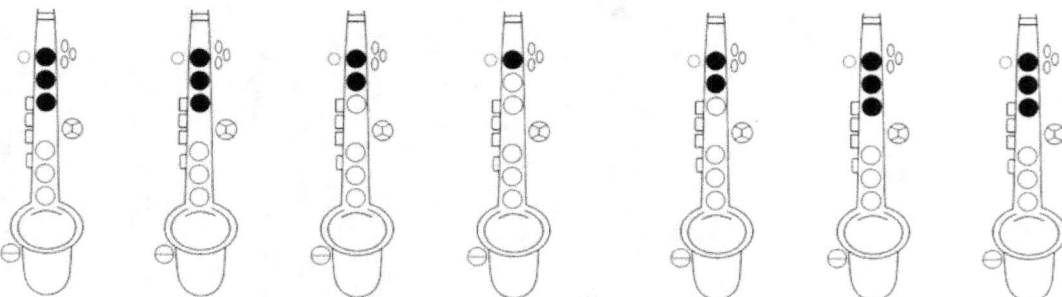

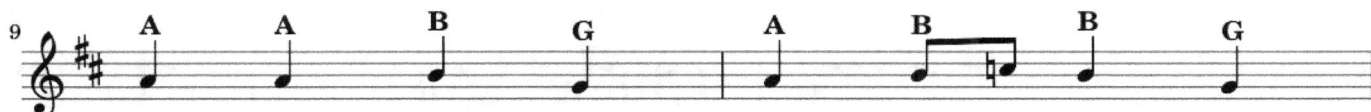

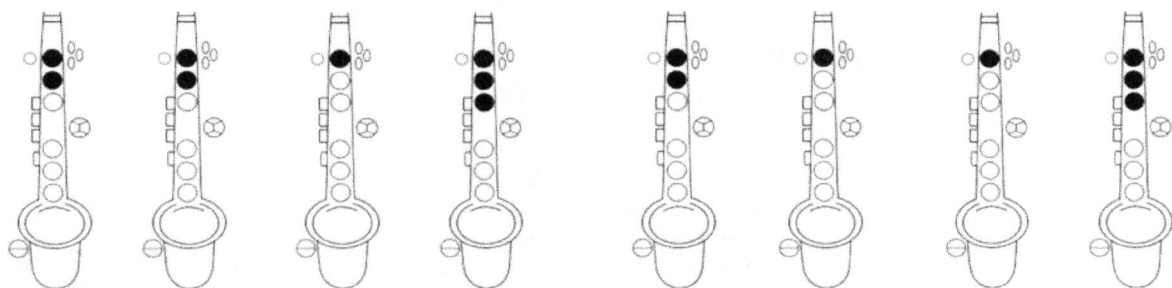

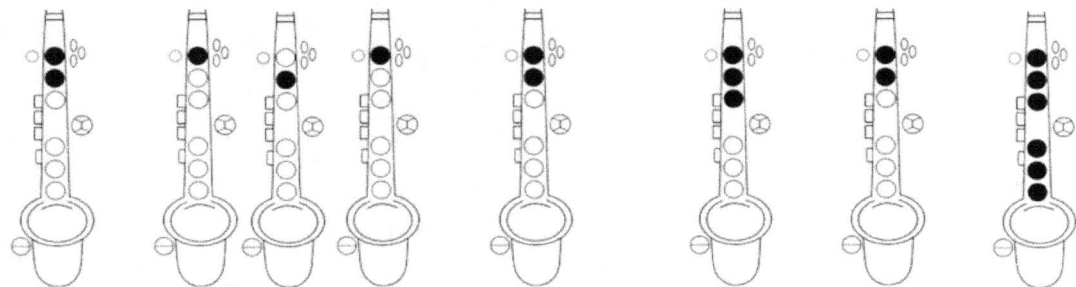

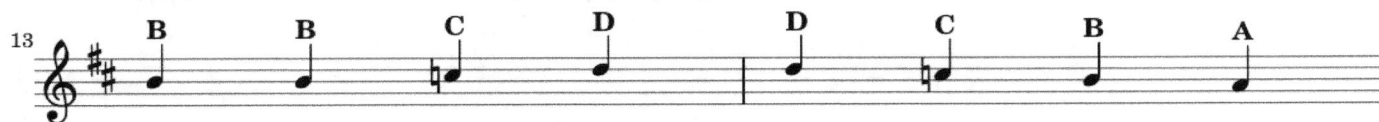

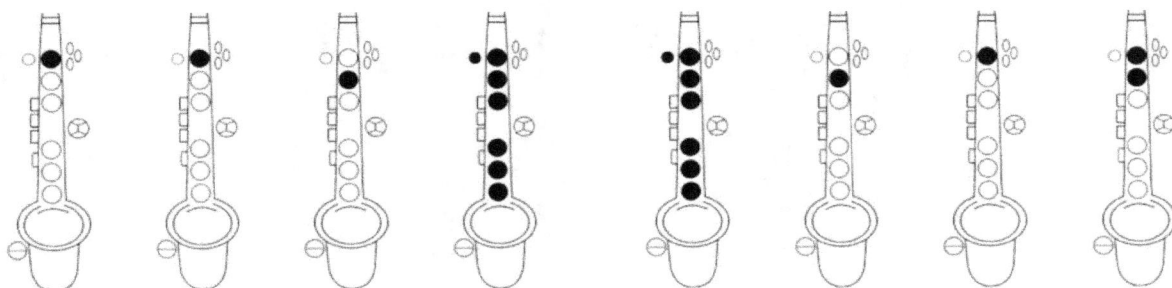

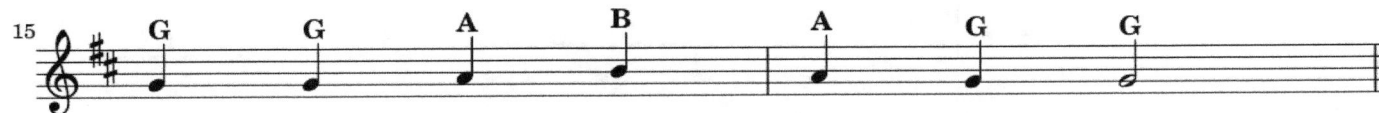

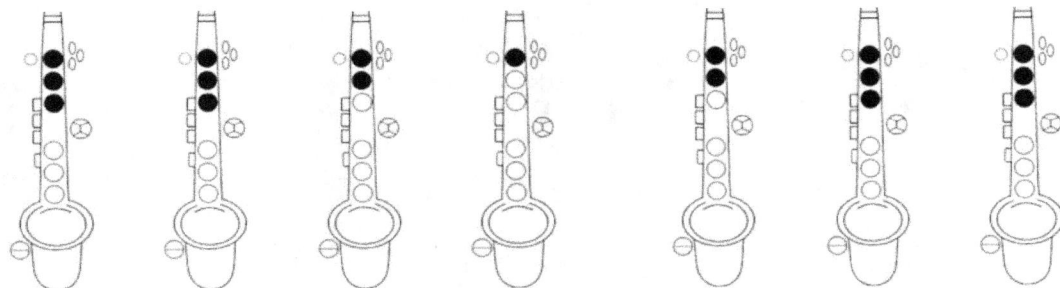

She'll Be Comin' 'Round the Mountain

Traditional American (19th Century)

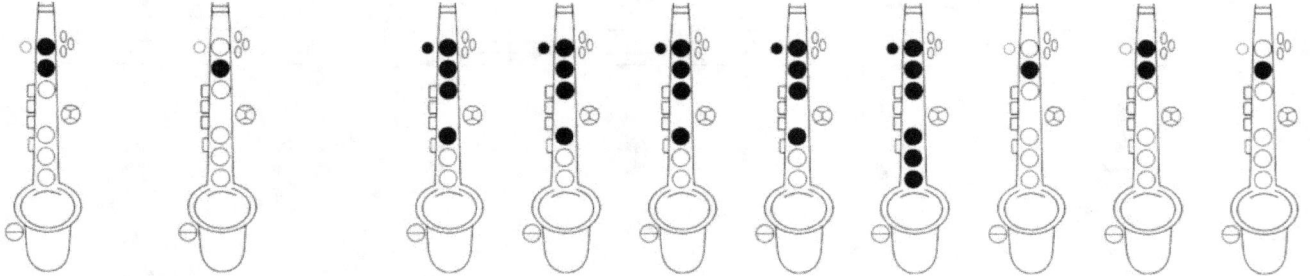

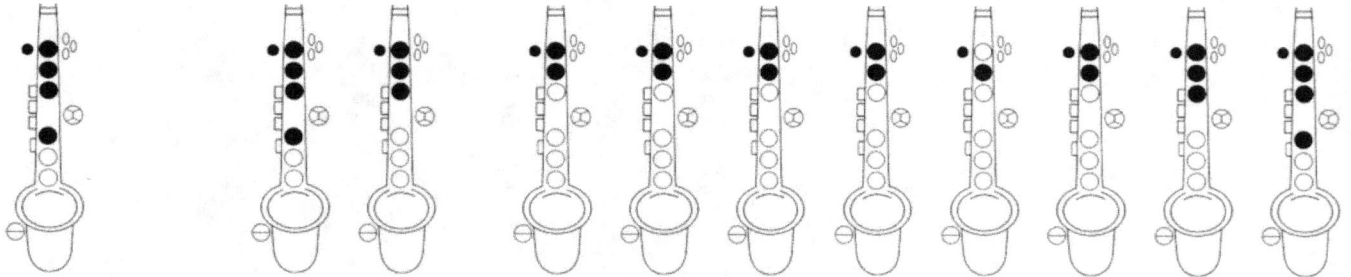

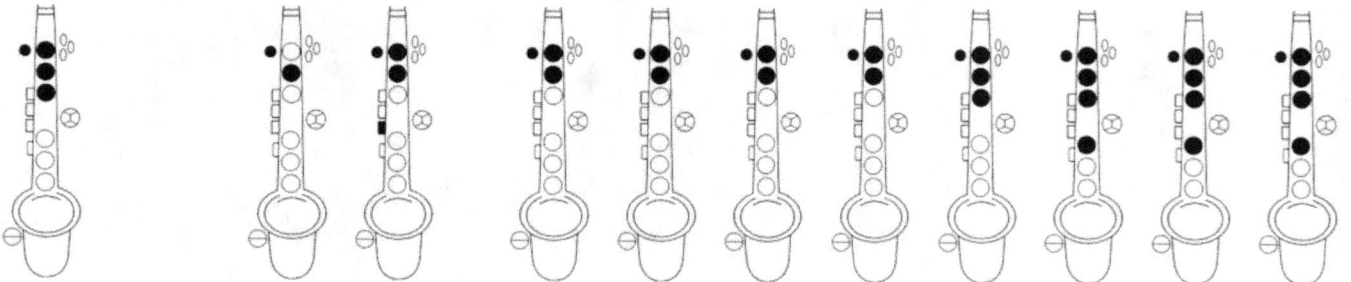

This song is arranged as a high note challenge.

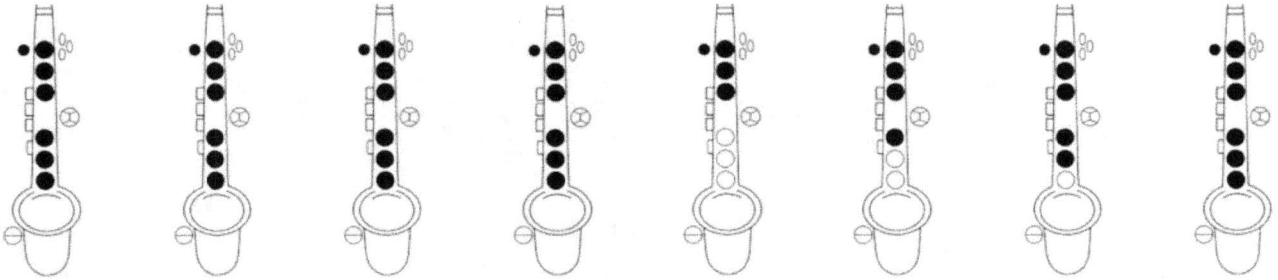

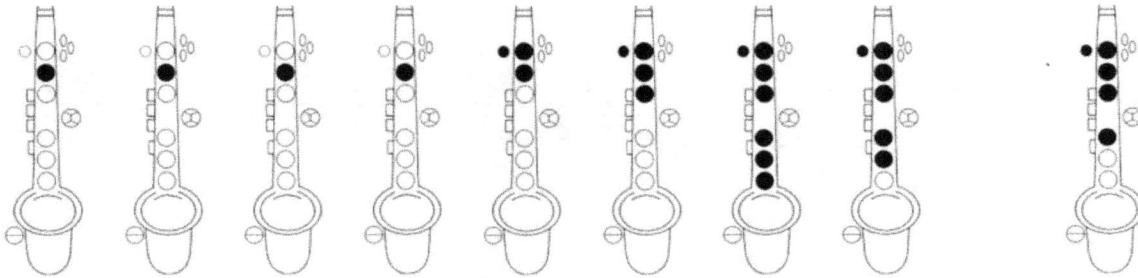

Scan the QR Code

to Listen to the song!

When the Saints Go Marching In

Traditional American (19th Century)

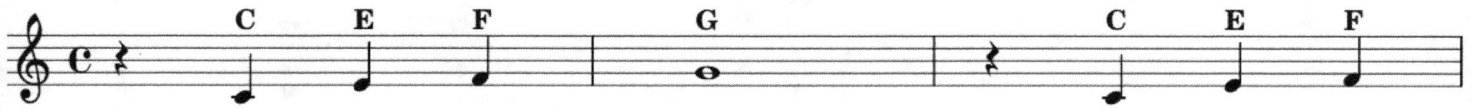

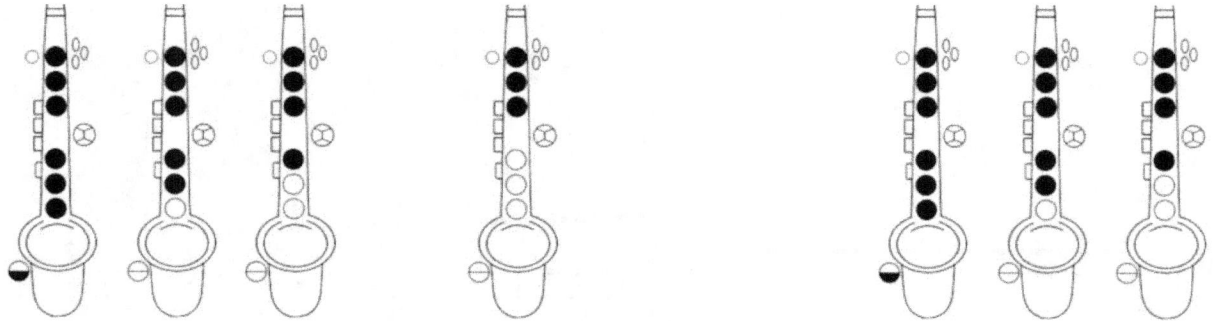

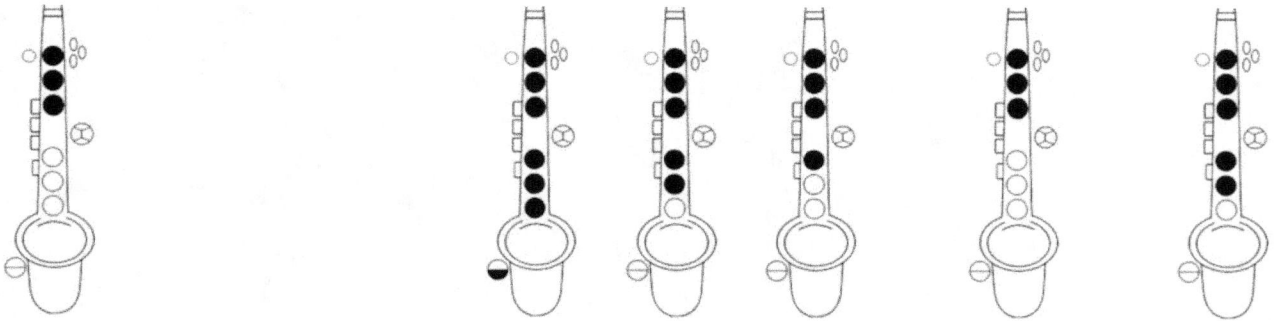

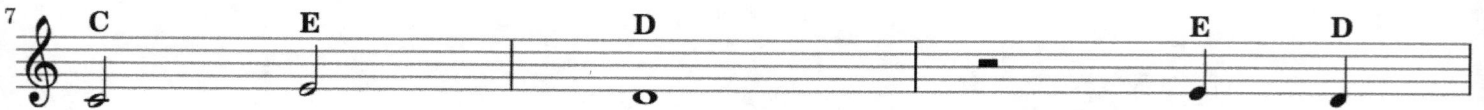

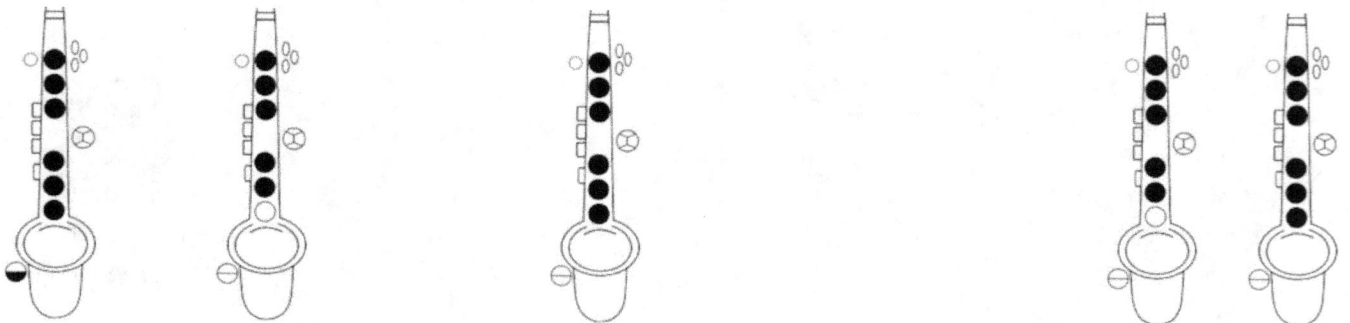

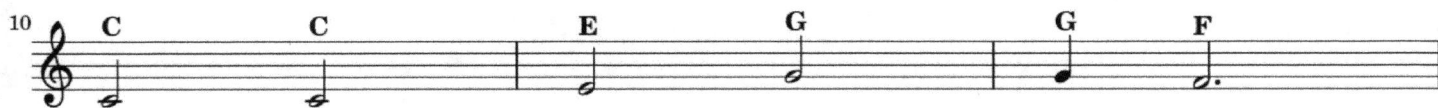

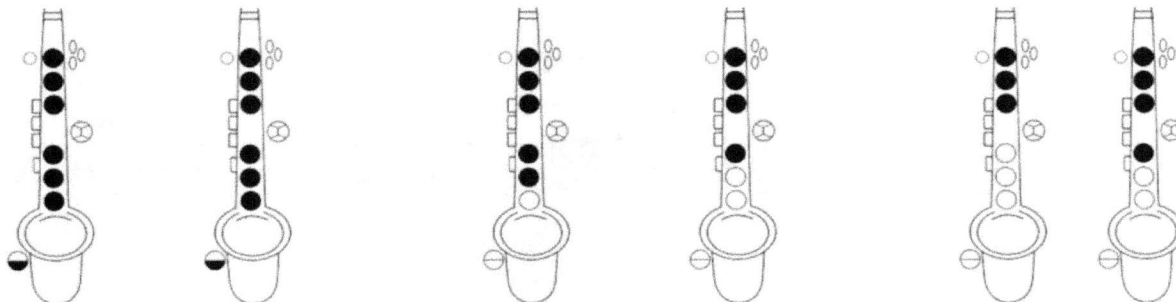

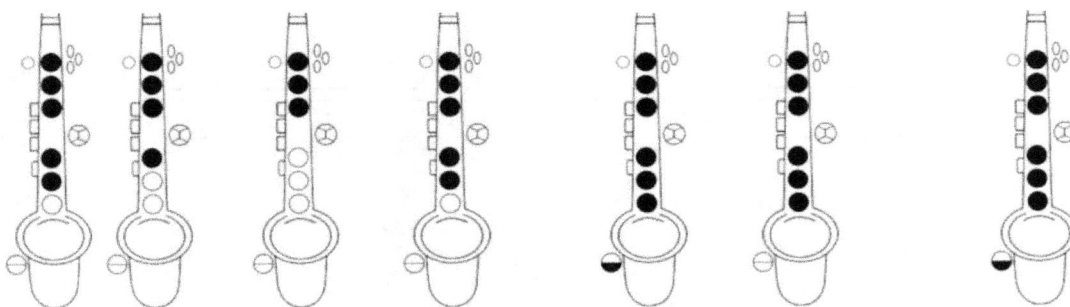

Scan the
QR Code

to Listen to
the song!

3
Amazing Grace

William Walker (1835)

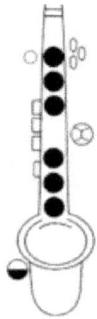

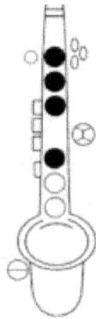

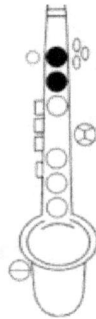

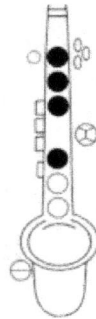

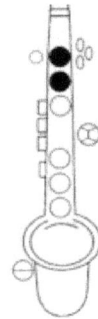

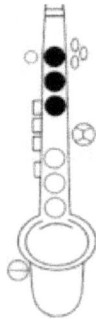

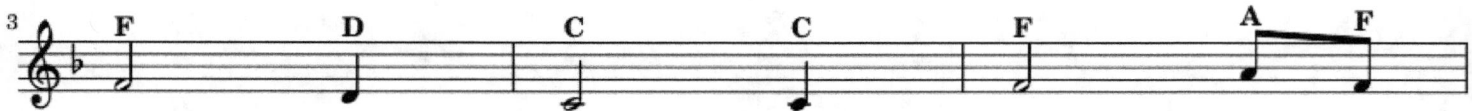

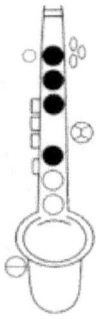

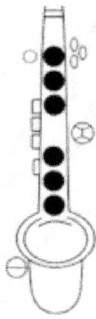

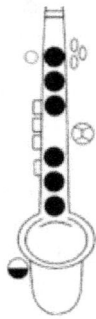

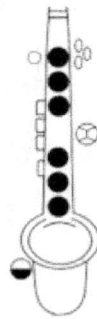

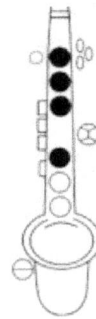

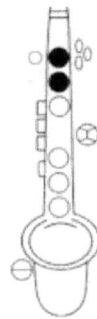

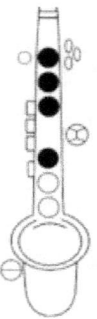

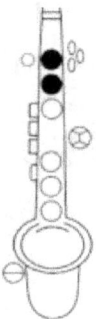

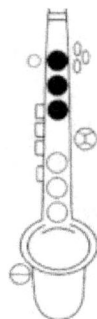

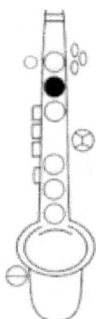

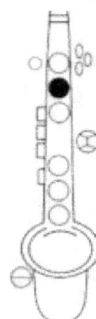

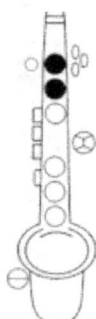

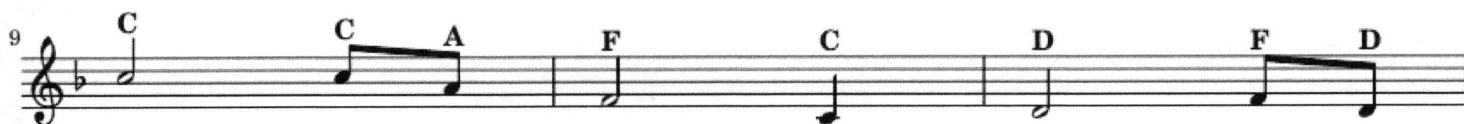

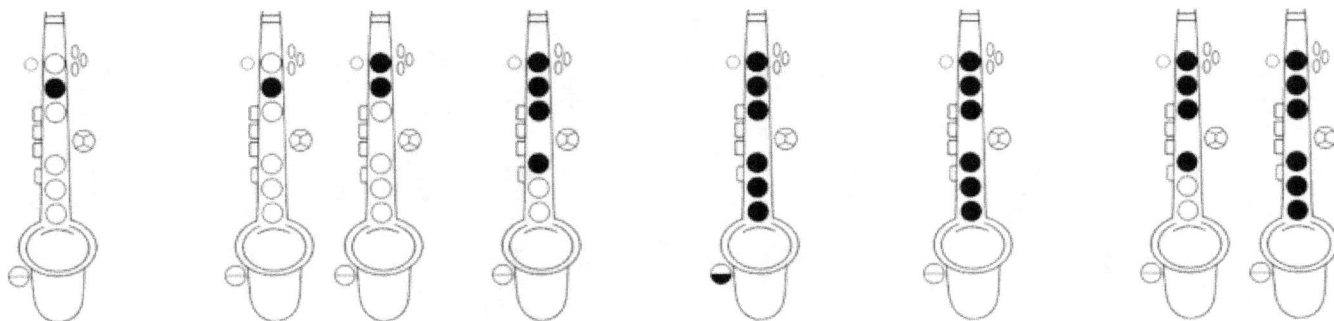

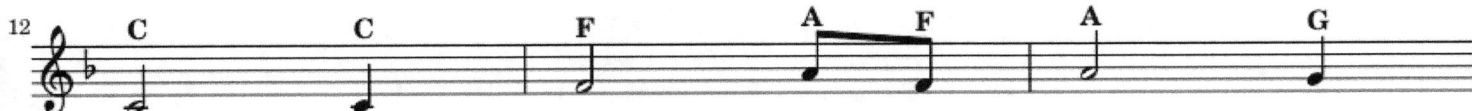

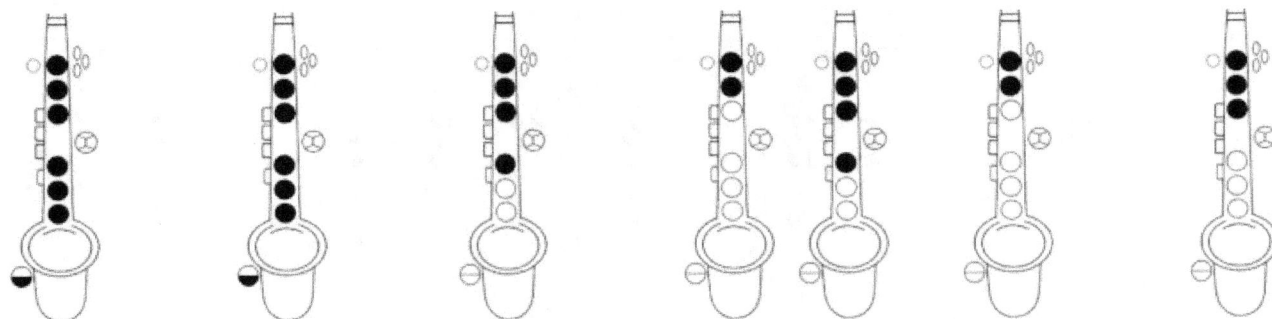

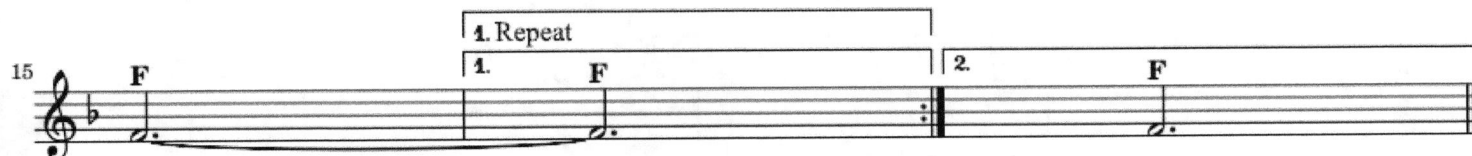

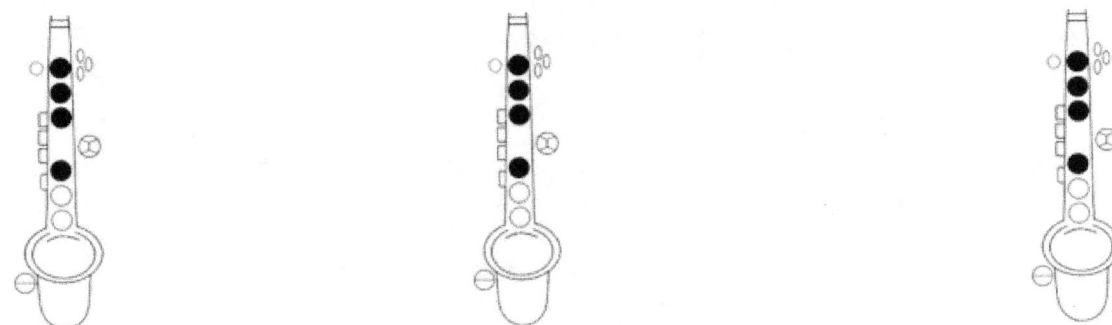

Scan the QR Code to Listen to the song!

Jingle Bells

J. Pierpont (1857)

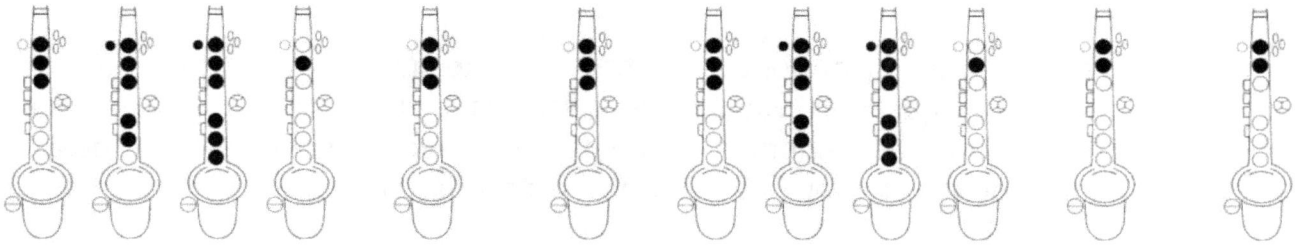

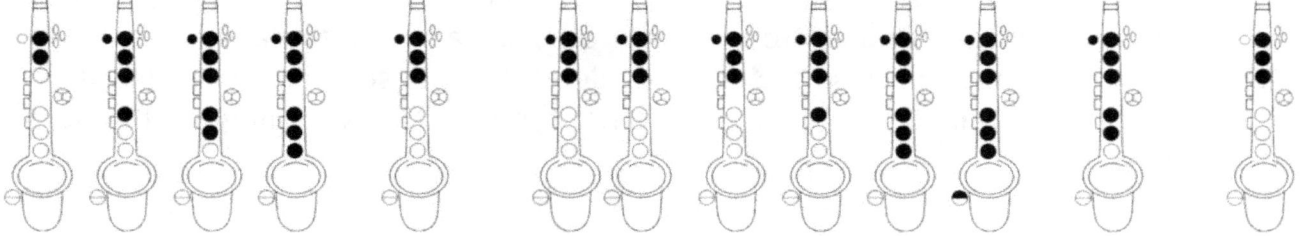

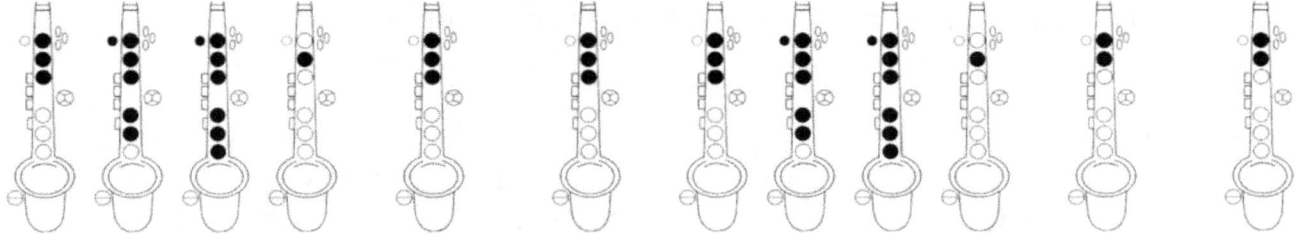

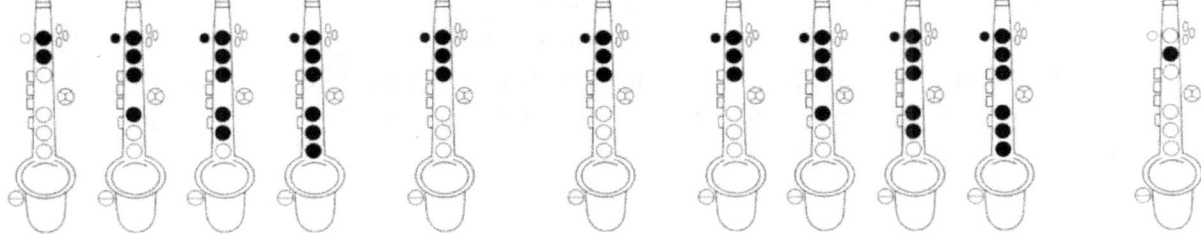

This song is arranged as a jazzy note challenge.

Scan the QR Code

to Listen to the song!

Tips for Playing Alto Saxophone

Learning to play the alto saxophone is exciting and, like any new skill, it takes time, patience, and steady practice. If you are just getting started, these tips will help you build good habits from the beginning. Remember that every great player started as a beginner, so do not worry if your sound is not perfect right away.

Tip 1: Press the Keys Correctly
On the saxophone, each key controls a pad that must close tightly over a tone hole to make a clear sound. If a key is not pressed firmly enough, air can leak and cause squeaks or missing notes. Keep your fingers curved naturally, resting lightly on the pearls, which are the round key tops. When you press a key, use relaxed, even pressure, firm enough to close the pad completely but not so hard that your hands tense up. Practicing in front of a mirror can help you see that your fingers stay close to the keys.

Tip 2: Keep Your Hands Relaxed
It is easy to tighten your hands and fingers when learning something new. But stiffness makes it harder to move smoothly and quickly. Think of playing the sax as similar to typing on a keyboard. Your fingers should move lightly and easily, without strain. Shake out your hands from time to time and remind yourself to stay loose while you play.

Tip 3: Take It Slow
When you are learning a new scale or song, it can be tempting to rush. Going too fast too soon often leads to uneven notes and bad habits. Start slowly and focus on making every note clear and steady. As you repeat the motion, your fingers will learn the pattern, and speed will come naturally. Accuracy comes first, then speed.

Fun Fact: Alto Saxophone and Other Woodwinds
The alto saxophone is part of the woodwind family, and its fingerings are very similar to those on other saxophones and even the clarinet. Once you know your basic notes on alto sax, you already have a head start on learning tenor sax, baritone sax, or other woodwind instruments.

Make Music
Starting the alto saxophone is the beginning of a great musical adventure. Keep practicing, take short breaks, and enjoy every bit of progress you make. Each new note, scale, and song brings you closer to playing the music you love. Stay patient, have fun, and make music proudly.

E♭ Alto Saxophone Fingering Chart

The E♭ Alto Saxophone fingering chart begins with the note A#3-B♭3 (A-sharp 3 equals B-flat 3), the lowest note playable on the instrument. Next, the chart rises step by step, showing flats (♭) and sharps (#), all the way up to F6. This fingering chart is presented as a **Chromatic Scale.**

A chromatic scale is a musical scale that goes up or down by half steps, the smallest steps in music. Think of playing every single note in order, without skipping any. Scan the QR code to listen to the whole scale from A#3-B♭3 to F6.

The numbers 3, 4, 5, and 6 are called octave numbers. Octave numbers are the numbers you see next to a note name, like C4 or F6. They tell you how high or low a note sounds on your instrument or in music. Each time you go from one C note to the next higher sounding C note, you move up one octave and the number increases by one. So, the number helps show which version of the note you're playing: low, middle, or high.

A#3-B♭3 to F4

E♭ Alto Saxophone Fingering Chart
F#4-G♭4 to F5

E♭ Alto Saxophone Fingering Chart
F#5-G♭5 to F6

21

F#5-G♭5   **G5**   **G#5-A♭5**   **A5**

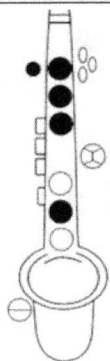 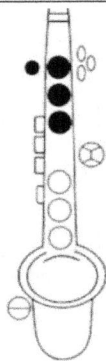 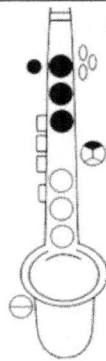 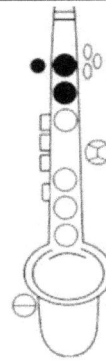

25

A#5-B♭5   **B5**   **C6**   **C#6-D♭6**

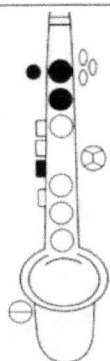 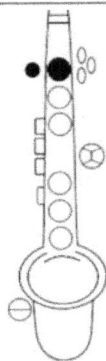 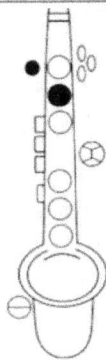 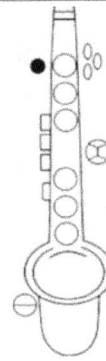

29

D6   **D#6-E♭6**   **E6**   **F6**

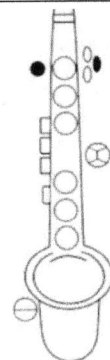 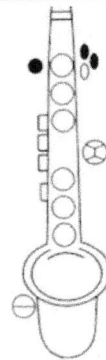 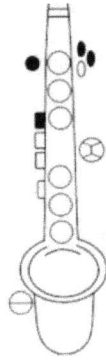 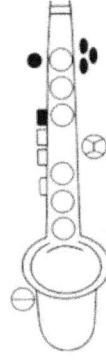

E♭ Alto Saxophone History

The alto saxophone is part of the saxophone family, a group of instruments invented by Adolphe Sax in the 1840s. Sax was a Belgian musician and instrument maker who wanted to create something that combined the power of brass instruments with the smooth sound of woodwinds. He used a metal body like a trumpet but added a single reed mouthpiece like a clarinet. The result was a new kind of instrument that could blend beautifully with both brass and woodwinds.

Sax patented his invention in 1846, creating a whole family of saxophones, from the tiny sopranino to the giant contrabass. The alto saxophone, tuned in E♭, became one of the most popular because of its comfortable size, wide range, and warm, singing tone.

At first, the saxophone was used mainly in military bands, especially in France and Belgium. Over time, composers began to include it in classical music, and by the early 1900s, it found a new home in jazz. Great players like Charlie Parker, Cannonball Adderley, and Paul Desmond helped make the alto sax famous for its expressive sound and emotional power.

Today, the alto saxophone is played in concert bands, jazz ensembles, marching bands, and even in pop and rock music. Its voice can be smooth and mellow or bright and bold, making it one of the most versatile instruments in the world.

Did You Know?
The saxophone is made of brass, but it's actually a woodwind instrument. That's because the sound comes from a vibrating reed, not from buzzing lips like a trumpet or trombone.

E♭ Alto Saxophone

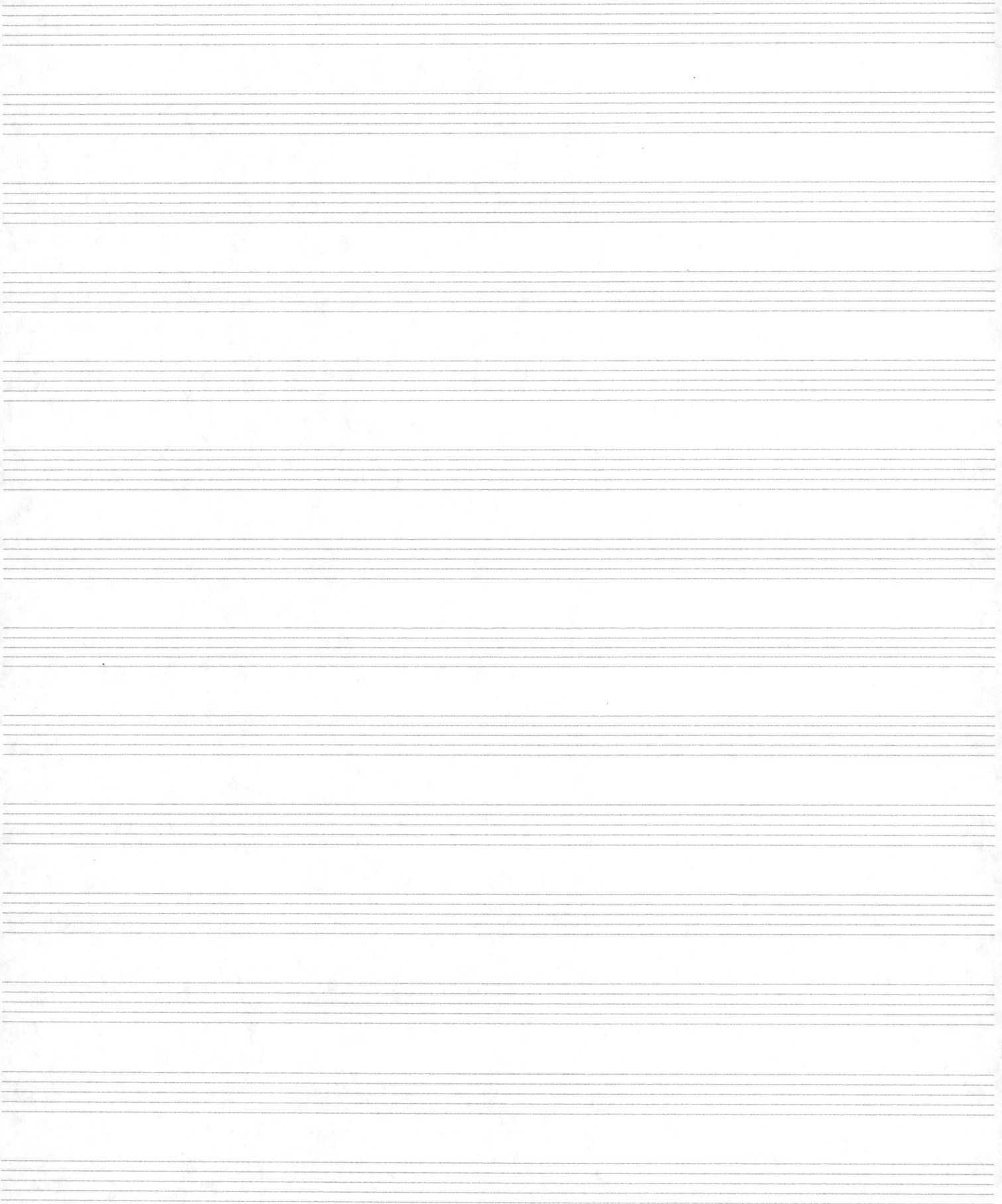

www.ingramcontent.com/pod-product-compliance
Lightning Source LLC
LaVergne TN
LVHW081336060426
835513LV00014B/1310